SARATOGA

Brain Disorders

GRAY
MATTER

GRAY
MATTER

Brain Disorders

Brian C. Hains

CHELSEA HOUSE
P U B L I S H E R S
A Haights Cross Communications Company ®
P h i l a d e l p h i a

CHELSEA HOUSE PUBLISHERS

VP, NEW PRODUCT DEVELOPMENT Sally Cheney
DIRECTOR OF PRODUCTION Kim Shinners
CREATIVE MANAGER Takeshi Takahashi
MANUFACTURING MANAGER Diann Grasse
PRODUCTION EDITOR Noelle Nardone
PHOTO EDITOR Sarah Bloom

STAFF FOR BRAIN DISORDERS

PROJECT MANAGEMENT Dovetail Content Solutions
DEVELOPMENTAL EDITOR Carol Field
PROJECT MANAGER Pat Mrozek
PHOTO EDITOR Margaret Mary Anderson
SERIES AND COVER DESIGNER Terry Mallon
LAYOUT Maryland Composition Company, Inc.

A Haights Cross Communications ✦ Company ®

www.chelseahouse.com

First Printing

10 9 8 7 6 5 4 3 2 1

Library of Congress Cataloging-in-Publication Data

Hains, Bryan.
    Brain disorders / Bryan Hains.
    p. cm. — (Gray matter series)
Includes bibliographical references and index.
    ISBN 0-7910-8513-9
1. Brain—Diseases. I. Title. II. Gray matter.
RC386.2.H35 2005
616.8—dc22

2005015851

All links, web addresses, and Internet search terms were checked and verified to be correct at
the time of publication. Because of the dynamic nature of the web, some addresses and links
may have changed since publication and may no longer be valid.

Contents

1 | Alzheimer's Disease

Imagine that at age 70, after a full and flourishing life, you slowly and frustratingly begin to lose track of where you are, why you are doing something, or who your loved ones are. Your day-to-day reality takes on a different meaning, one foreign and mysterious to you. Eventually, you find yourself in a nursing home, unable to feed yourself or even communicate, completely shut off from the world because of an abnormality deep within your brain. This is the course of a brain disorder called **Alzheimer's disease** (AD).

PREVALENCE AND IMPLICATIONS

Within the United States alone, it is estimated that 4 million people suffer from AD or a related disorder. Approximately 10% of Americans over the age of 65, and nearly 50% of those over 85, have AD. The probability of developing Alzheimer's disease increases with advancing age. Typically, symptoms of AD begin at age 60–65, but a small percentage of people in their 40s, 50s, and early 60s also have signs and symptoms of AD (see "Alzheimer's Disease: Auguste D" box).

The impact of AD on mortality rates and economic factors is staggering. AD is the fourth leading cause of death among adults, and is a major cause of declining quality of

Alzheimer's Disease: Auguste D.

The symptoms of what is now known as AD were first described in detail by a German physician named Dr. Alois Alzheimer. In 1901, Alzheimer began to treat a 51-year-old woman named Auguste D. Her condition deteriorated steadily from memory loss, difficulty with speech, confusion, suspicion, agitation, and wandering. She also became bedridden, incontinent, and unaware of her surroundings. In 1905, after her death, Alzheimer performed an autopsy of Auguste D. He found that her brain had shriveled, and that neurons had disappeared when he examined tissue sections of her brain under a microscope. He also discovered the presence of thread-like spindle-shaped objects that he called "neurofibrillary tangles" and vicious-looking blobs described as "senile plaques," similar to those previously found in the brains of very old people. It is because of his initial characterization that the disease has been named Alzheimer's disease.

Dr. Alois Alzheimer, the doctor who first described the condition we now know as Alzheimer's disease.

life and nursing home admissions. The typical life expectancy after the onset of symptoms of AD is 8–10 years. In terms of cost, AD is the third most expensive disease to manage, after heart disease and cancer, with an average lifetime cost per patient of $174,000. The United States spends more than $100 billion a year directly on medical care and indirectly on lost productivity related to AD.

SIGNS AND SYMPTOMS

Alzheimer's disease is an irreversible, progressive, **neurodegenerative** disease of the brain that slowly destroys memory and thinking skills. The term *neurodegenerative* refers to the fact that degeneration takes place within the cells of the nervous system. Over the course of many years, AD renders a person unable to carry out the simplest daily tasks, and reliant on the help of others to survive. AD is the most common form of age-related **dementia**. Dementia is the loss of the normal ability to form new short-term memories, the loss of previously formed long-term memories, and impairments related to abstract thinking and judgment. These brain functions are predominantly governed by the **hippocampus**, frontal lobe, and basal forebrain.

People with AD suffer mainly from impaired short-term memory formation and orientation (awareness of location and direction), limitations in concentration, planning, and judgment, as well as personality changes. For example, people with AD may revert to a childlike mental state as the disease progresses, or walk around the streets aimlessly, apparently unaware of their location, their address, or the purpose of their wanderings. Later in the course of the disease, losses in sensory perception, speech, and movement become apparent. In the final stages of AD, primary physiological functions such as eating and excretion are affected.

PATHOLOGICAL CHANGES

Scientists are beginning to understand the complex changes in the brain that occur in AD. But before we explore these changes, the cellular architecture of the brain must first be described. The brain is made up of approximately 10^{11} (100,000,000,000) **neurons**, specialized cells of the body that exist within the brain, spinal cord, and peripheral nerves (the body's equivalent of electrical transmission wires). Neurons are electrically excitable cells that fire signals to other neurons and other cell types in the body, communicating messages. Messages are conducted along an **axon**, the long structure that emerges from the cell body of the neuron. Messages are received by other neurons through highly branched **dendrites**, as well as on neuronal cell bodies and axons. Each neuron receives connections from and makes connections to 1,000 to 10,000 other neurons through a specialized connection region called a **synapse**. In some areas of the body, these connections directly target muscles and are responsible for starting and maintaining muscular movement or other "simple" actions. In other parts of the nervous system, such as the frontal lobe and other areas of the brain and spinal cord, neurons construct sophisticated neural networks that are involved in processing complex information or directing higher functioning such as language production and comprehension, abstract thought, or creativity.

In adults, the number of neurons in the **cerebral cortex**, the outer "bark" of the brain, is approximately 22 billion. When we are born, our brains are nearly complete in terms of the maximum number of neurons, and over the course of our lifetime, neurons die off naturally, although recent research has shown that neurons can be born in specialized areas of the adult brain. In healthy adults, the rate of neuronal loss is 85,000 neurons per day (~31 million per year). This loss is a normal phenomenon and partially contributes to age-related changes in memory and cognitive function. In AD, however, this progression is

good pic

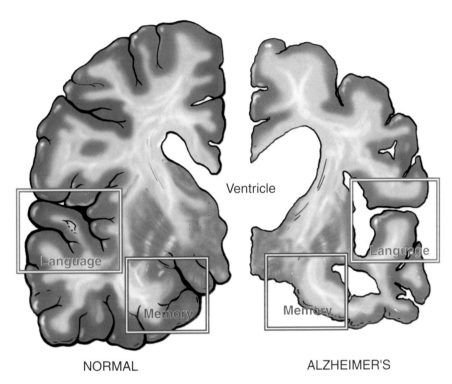

Ventricle

Language

Memory

Language

Memory

NORMAL   ALZHEIMER'S

Figure 1.1 AD results in changes in the cerebral cortex. The ventricles expand as brain tissue is lost.

dramatically accelerated and neuron loss is extensive within the cortex and other structures.

Advanced AD results in a brain that appears quite different from a normal brain. Because there is significant neuron loss in the cerebral cortex, the brain becomes smaller and its overall shape becomes more convoluted. The normal ridges and valleys of the cortex become more exaggerated as the cortex shrinks. In addition, the **ventricles**, hollow channels that bathe the brain in nutrient-rich fluids, expand as they take over areas of lost brain tissue. These changes are quite striking, and are easily seen by doctors looking at pictures of the brain (Figure 1.1).

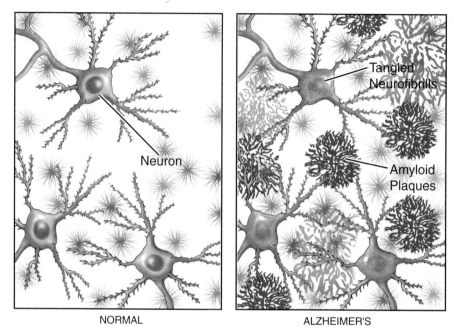

NORMAL   ALZHEIMER'S

Figure 1.2 Amyloid plaques and neurofibrillary tangles are the hallmarks of AD.

The brains of AD patients begin to appear shrunken as affected areas of the cortex begin to degenerate and collapse. The first area of the brain to undergo degeneration is often the hippocampus, which is involved in the formation of long-term memories. As a result, a person with AD experiences problems in memory processing.

Neuronal death is the end-stage of a number of pathological (abnormal) processes that take place in neurons within the brains of individuals with AD. The **amyloid plaques** and **neurofibrillary tangles** that form are thought to contribute to the degeneration of neurons and subsequent symptoms of AD, and are considered the pathological hallmarks that distinguish AD from other types of dementia (Figure 1.2).

In all cases of AD, toxic levels of **amyloid protein** accumulate and destroy brain regions next to the accumulation sites. The word *amyloid* is used to describe small protein fragments that are normally produced by all cells. In AD, however, the mechanisms that would normally break down and clear away amyloid protein fail. Because of this failure, amyloid proteins cluster into dense, insoluble fibrils (tangled, thread-like structures) that are deposited as amyloid plaques on both the inside and outside of neurons.

Amyloid plaques are made up mostly of beta amyloid protein, a small protein fragment that is cut from a larger protein called beta amyloid precursor protein (APP). Beta APP is normally present in the walls of cells within the body, and is not restricted to neurons. It is thought to play a role in neuronal growth and survival, and in helping injured neurons repair themselves. Cut beta amyloid protein clumps together to form the plaques that are characteristic of AD.

AD is also associated with the formation of neurofibrillary tangles. Neurofibrillary tangles consist of insoluble twisted fibers that are found on the inside of neurons. Neurons maintain their shape and structure by constructing an internal skeleton made of rigid fibers called **microtubules**. Microtubules also help the neuron shuttle supplies, energy sources, and building materials around within itself and its dendrite tree, axons, and synapses. Special proteins called **tau** work with microtubules and help maintain the stability and orientation of microtubules within the neuron. In AD brains, there is an abnormality of the tau protein that causes the microtubular structure to collapse. This results in the inability of the neuron to maintain healthy functioning and communication, and eventually results in neuronal death. In these shrunken degenerating neurons, tau protein accumulates. Tau abnormalities are also observed with other diseases that affect the nervous system. These diseases, called tauopathies, include supranuclear palsy, Pick's disease, and degeneration of the cerebral cortex and the **basal ganglia**, as with Parkinson's disease. These disorders have many symptoms in common, including dementia, as well as changes in thinking ability and personality. Despite these similarities, each disease has features that distinguish it from AD.

The relationships among beta APP, neurofibrillary tangles, and tau are not well established at this point. For example, it is unknown whether beta amyloid plaques cause AD or are by-products of the disease process. It may take years to understand how these changes come about and how the molecular and cellular features of AD interact.

CAUSES AND HERITABILITY

The causes of amyloid plaque accumulation and formation of neurofibrillary tangles in AD are unknown. There is probably not one single cause, but scientists believe that genetics may be important because AD tends to run in families. For example, mutations in **genes** located on **chromosomes** 1, 14, 19, and 21 are believed to play a role in AD, and abnormalities associated with a gene that encodes a protein called **apolipoprotein E** on chromosome 19 tend to be more common in people with familial AD than in the general population.

In Down's syndrome, also known as trisomy 21, all cells in the body have an extra copy of chromosome 21. In these individuals, amyloid plaques accumulate as in AD, but often the memory changes associated with AD are not present, which calls into question the idea of a single factor determining the development and course of AD.

Because family members are generally exposed to the same environment, it is difficult to determine whether the causes of AD are purely genetic, or whether they are influenced by environmental factors such as geographic location or diet. Much research is being carried out to try to understand the interrelationship between genes, environmental factors, and susceptibility to AD. In twin studies, identical twins have a higher rate of both twins developing AD (78%) than nonidentical twins (39%), suggesting a strong genetic component.

TREATMENT AND OUTLOOK

To date, nothing can be done to slow the progression or reverse the deficits caused by AD. Not enough is known about the causes of AD to enable the development of drugs that interfere with the disease's progression. There are drugs, however, that can reduce the severity of AD symptoms in people in the early stages of AD. These drugs are most helpful in preventing memory loss, dementia, and other cognitive-behavioral functions, and can greatly improve the lives of people with AD and their families. Typically, these compounds slow the progress of symptoms by about 6–12 months.

Research is ongoing for a drug or treatment that can prevent the onset of AD in individuals with a genetic predisposition. Recent findings show that vitamin E and anti-inflammatory drugs can be useful. These drugs are able to temporarily slow the progression of AD, but cannot prevent or stop the disease from developing. Studies also suggest that hormone replacement therapy in postmenopausal women may halt the progression of AD, but these results are controversial.

■ **Learn more about Alzheimer's disease** Search the Internet for *Alzheimer's disease* and *dementia.*

2 | Parkinson's Disease

Deep within the core of the brain lies highly specialized interconnected networked circuitry responsible for the initiation of complex motor actions. This collection of nuclei processes sensory information regarding limb position, balance, movement direction and speed, and body mechanics, and compiles this information and sends commands to the motor cortex, from which signals are sent down to the spinal cord for execution.

Any dysfunction within the components of the motor command system results in abnormal motor output. For instance, blocking impulses as they travel down the spinal cord will prevent any movements that are controlled by the cortex. Altering movement messages before they reach the cortex will produce confused commands and physical symptoms of a disease known as **Parkinson's disease** (PD).

PD is a common brain disorder affecting approximately 1.5 million Americans (5% of the total U.S. population). Between 50,000 and 60,000 new patients are diagnosed every year. After the age of 50, however, the prevalence of PD rises to 1% of the population. Unrecognized early symptoms of the disease may be present in as many as 10% of those over 60 years of age, although only 0.5% of people over the age of 65 are diagnosed with PD.

PD was first described in 1817 by James Parkinson in an article titled "An Essay on the Shaking Palsy." Parkinson characterized the disease as ". . . an involuntary tremulous motion, with lessened muscular power, in parts not in action and even when supported; with a propensity to bend the trunk forwards, and to pass from a walking to a running pace, the senses and intellects being uninjured."

SIGNS AND SYMPTOMS

As with Alzheimer's disease, PD is a progressive degenerative disorder of the central nervous system, and presents in a subtle manner. The major symptoms of PD are **bradykinesia, tremor,** and rigidity (Figure 2.1).

Bradykinesia is a slowing of the speed of initiation and execution of both purposeful and automatic movements. Gross movements, such as rising from of a chair and walking, and fine movements, such as tapping the fingers, are slowed. Handwriting becomes small and imprecise. Performing rapid repetitive movements becomes difficult for people with PD. When a person with PD walks, the gait is slowed and the feet tend to shuffle along the floor as if weighted down. In addition, the upper body appears to lean forward in the direction of movement, indicating changes in **postural reflexes**. With changes in postural reflexes, patients appear to be leaning too far forward when they walk. This results from failures in rapid adjustments of large opposing muscle groups that maintain proper balance and body positioning. Additionally, the faces of people with PD tend to be "masked" and expressionless as a result of slowed voluntary facial movements.

Resting tremor is shaking that occurs in relaxed muscles, typically in outer extremities such as the hands. Fingers demonstrate a regular twitching motion while at rest, often referred to as "pill-rolling tremor." This tremor results from activation of

Figure 2.1 The late Pope John Paul II, shown here, was affected by PD. A person with PD exhibits postural deficits and appears to be leaning forward in the direction of movement. When walking, the gait is slowed and the feet tend to shuffle as if weighted down.

opposing muscle groups that alternate between contraction and relaxation.

Muscular rigidity in PD is often described as "cogwheel rigidity" because of the increased muscle tone (tension) that feels ratchet-like when resistance is applied. Repeated movements of arm and leg joints result in muscular stiffness, and movements take on a jerky quality.

People with PD may also have trouble starting new movements and have a reduction of voluntary movements, which is called **akinesia**.

PATHOLOGICAL CHANGES

The mechanisms underlying PD are fairly well known. PD is caused by the progressive loss of neurons that produce a **neurotransmitter** called **dopamine** in a part of the brain called the **substantia nigra**. The substantia nigra is part of a collection of nuclei within the core or center of the brain that make up the basal ganglia. The basal ganglia, working with the cerebral cortex, serve to initiate and control body movements.

Substantia nigra is a Latin term that means "black substance." If a brain is removed and sliced, this substantia nigra appears dark in color because of the presence of a pigment known as melanin. These neurons produce a chemical messenger (a neurotransmitter) called dopamine, used to convey signals between neurons. Approximately 80% of all dopamine in the brain is produced in the substantia nigra, and it is used by nigral neurons to relay messages between the substantia nigra and other clusters of neurons that make up the basal ganglia. Dopamine is one of the most important neurotransmitters used by the brain to control muscular activity.

The production, release, and reabsorption of neurotransmitters are highly regulated by neurons and supporting cells. Any fluctuation or change in any of these processes results in variations in the intended message being communicated between neurons. Because this system is very finely balanced, subtle changes result in major changes in output. In the case of PD, in which dopamine levels are decreased, the delicate equilibrium is disrupted and motor signals become erroneus. Reduction in the levels of dopamine results in the inability of patients to have precise control over muscular movements in a normal manner. When the amount of dopamine made by the substantia nigra drops to 80% below normal production levels, PD symptons start to appear.

The basal ganglia can be thought of as a processing and command center for voluntary movement (Figure 2.2). Information is received by this cluster of nuclei from the **primary motor cortex** at the surface of the brain, which translates volitional motor "thoughts" into executable commands. The basal ganglia then process these commands, and route them to the thalamus, which relays them down to the spinal cord, where connections are made to muscle groups. The net effect of the normally functioning cortex-basal ganglia output circuit is excitatory.

The basal ganglia is a group of interconnected nuclei (dedicated clusters of neurons that all perform a similar function). These nuclei are: the **globus pallidus** (internal and external segments), the **subthalamic nucleus**, the substantia nigra (pars compacta and reticulata), and the **striatum** (caudate nucleus and putamen).

Inputs from the cerebral cortex are received by the striatum. The striatum also receives inputs from the substantia nigra (where dopamine is used as the neurotransmitter), and this pathway is referred to as the **nigrostriatal pathway**. In this connection, dopamine is both excitatory (making neurons more likely to fire) and inhibitory (making neurons less likely to fire), depending on the type of **receptor** it binds to, and is the connec-

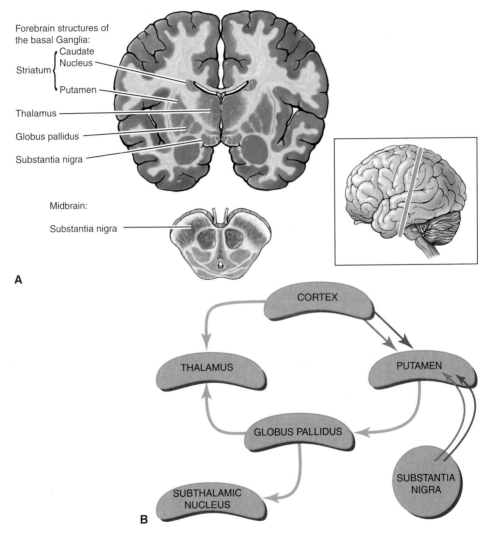

Figure 2.2 This cross section of the brain shows the basal ganglia from the axis shown in the inset at left. The structures within the basal ganglia **(A)** can be thought of as the processing and command center for voluntary movement. **(B)** This diagram shows the path followed when information is processed through the basal ganglia and routed through the thalamus to then be relayed to the spinal cord.

tion most directly influenced by PD. Because dopamine can exert both excitatory and inhibitory influences on the striatum, the balance of inputs is very delicate. The striatum sends projections to the globus pallidus (both internal and external components), which then sends projections to the thalamus for output, and to the subthalamic nuclei for further processing.

The overall function of dopamine is to dampen the output of the entire basal ganglia. But when dopamine levels are reduced, as in PD, the output of basal ganglia circuitry is left unchecked. Specifically, there is decreased input to the caudate. As a result, there is increased inhibition at the globus pallidus that leads to tremor, rigidity, and spasticity (Figure 2.3). This increased tone of the basal ganglia causes increased muscle tension and tremor. Downstream structures controlled by the basal ganglia, such as the thalamus and the loops back to the motor cortex, are inhibited, resulting in reduced motor behavior. This reduction in motor activity is consistent with bradykinesia (see "MPTP: Bad Heroin" box).

TREATMENT

The management of PD symptoms may at first seem fairly straightforward, with the most obvious method being simply to restore normal levels of dopamine in PD brains. Dopamine replacement therapy was first tried in the 1970s and found to be extremely effective.

The first drug of this type was known as **L-DOPA**. Unlike dopamine, L-DOPA freely passes through the blood-brain barrier (a tight network of membranes that does not allow drugs or potentially toxic substances to pass into the brain from the circulatory system). As a dopamine precursor molecule, L-DOPA is taken up selectively and converted into dopamine by remaining dopaminergic neurons, and used in the same manner as dopamine.

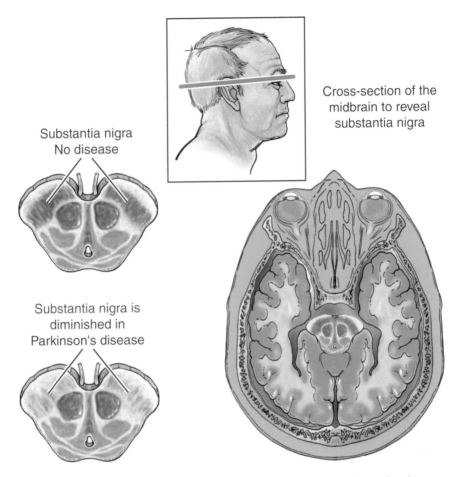

Substantia nigra
No disease

Cross-section of the
midbrain to reveal
substantia nigra

Substantia nigra is
diminished in
Parkinson's disease

Figure 2.3 A cross-section of the midbrain showing the subtantia nigra. In PD, dopamine-producing neurons of the subtantia nigra are lost.

Other ways to increase dopamine levels are to influence other steps in dopamine synthesis, release, and reabsorption into neurons after release and receptor binding. For example, deprenyl, a compound that selectively inhibits the enzyme (**monoamine oxidase B**) responsible for dopamine breakdown after release prolongs the activity of synaptically released dopamine. Inhibition of dopamine metabolism has the result of mimicking the higher-

MPTP: Bad Heroin

Insights into the mechanisms underlying PD were obtained in a surprising way in the early 1980s. The careless synthesis of an illegal heroin-like drug contained a contaminating compound called 4-phenyl-1,2,3,6-tetrahydropyridine (MPTP). This chemical was found to cause Parkinson-like symptoms in users. After ingestion, MPTP is converted to a neurotoxic substance called MPP+ that is taken up by neurons within the substantia nigra and results in the death of dopamine-containing neurons. The same enzyme that recycles used synaptic dopamine after release by transporting it back into neurons also facilitates the entry of MPP+. MPTP is currently used to destroy nigral neurons selectively and to produce an experimental model of PD in monkeys, to help researchers better understand and treat human PD.

The addicts shown here experienced PD-like symptoms after taking MPTP and are commonly referred to as the "frozen addicts."

concentration release by a larger number of healthy dopamine neurons.

Drugs that activate the same receptor sites as dopamine (called **agonists**) are also successful in reducing the symptoms of PD. But because these drugs can bind preferentially to excitatory or inhibitory receptors in the striatum, their successful adaptation is challenging. Also, because tolerance to these drugs develops over time, their doses must be constantly increased, which allows them to activate other dopamine receptors in the body and produce unwanted side effects. Because the gut contains many dopamine receptors, high-dose agonist administration results in nausea, vomiting, and diarrhea, which are difficult for patients to tolerate.

Recently, a surgical technique known as **deep brain stimulation** was developed to treat severe cases of PD. With the patient under anesthesia, a very thin wire electrode is inserted through the skull and brain into the subthalamic nucleus. A thin cable connected to the electrode is then threaded to the chest, where a pacemaker-like control device is implanted just under the skin. During times of extreme tremor, the patient can activate the pacemaker, which electrically stimulates the subthalamic nucleus. Stimulation immediately and dramatically stops tremor activity; however, bradykinesia and rigidity persist.

Currently, there is no known way to stop the degeneration of nigral neurons, and medical management of PD can only prolong the lives of those stricken with PD.

■ **Learn more about Parkinson's disease** Search the Internet for *postural reflex, parkinsonian,* or *James Parkinson.*

3 | Huntington's Disease

The appearance of a person with **Huntington's disease** (HD) is quite striking. Approximately 300 years ago, people who showed symptoms of HD were executed! In Salem, Massachusetts, a town known in the young American colonies for its witch hunts and subsequent executions, a number of women were put to death in the 1690s because they were thought to be possessed by the devil.

These possessions were "evidenced" by the choreiform movements exhibited by the women. Chorea consists of spasmodic, involuntary muscle jerks and twitches. When these muscle movements occur in the face, they look like grimacing. Individuals may also raise and lower their shoulders uncontrollably, and flex and extend their fingers in a rhythmic manner. The word *chorea* comes from a Greek word meaning "chorus" or a group of dancers. In the 1300s, it was also used to describe the behavior of European people with a number of disorders, including the "dancing mania" and the black plague, during which people were said to be consumed by the dance of St. Vitus. Historically, HD was called Huntington's chorea, but this name is no longer used.

SIGNS AND SYMPTOMS

HD was initially characterized in 1872 by an American physician named George Huntington, who published a short but classic paper titled "On Chorea." In this paper, Huntington described a hereditary nervous system disorder that included a tendency toward insanity and an expression of abnormal movements:

> The movements gradually increase when muscles hitherto unaffected take on the spasmodic action, until every muscle in the body becomes affected (excepting the involuntary ones). . . . As the disease progresses the mind becomes more or less impaired, in many accounting to insanity, while in others mind and body gradually fail until death relieves them of their suffering.

There seems to be a genetic predisposition to HD. Symptoms of HD start at approximately age 35, but in some cases do not appear until later. Most of the time, cases of earlier onset are associated with more severe disease. By the time symptoms appear, many people have already started families. Therefore, it may be too late to avoid passing the HD gene to their children. The prevalence of HD in the United States is about 5 cases per 100,000 people. HD is a progressive disorder that usually leads to death 15–20 years after the onset of neurological or psychological impairment.

Early disease-related symptoms involve mood disturbances, including problems with memory, common forgetfulness, and irritability (possibly resulting from frustration over the loss of memory). After a few years, these deficits become more pronounced and patients eventually experience more severe dementia and lack of coherent thought, or the ability to organize and regulate impulses.

Because HD is primarily a disorder affecting movement, choreiform motions are perhaps the most obvious sign of HD (Figure 3.1). These movements are not under the individual's control and may occur without provocation at any time. Typically, there are jerky displacements of short duration affecting the limbs and the face, and the movements are said to resemble

Figure 3.1 This illustration shows patients suffering from chorea, a common symptom of HD. Patients with chorea exhibit jerky, involuntary movements of the shoulders, hips, and face. This condition is sometimes called St. Vitus's dance or St. Guy's dance.

semi-purposeful actions that never flow to completion. An example of an initial choreiform movement sequence is that of clumsy simulated piano-playing motions of the fingers, hands, and arms. Later on in the course of the disease, these movements affect the torso and core muscle groups, causing the classic dancing walk. Despite the appearance of an uncoordinated gait, these patients are able to maintain correct balance. People with HD also appear to assume abnormal body positions when still.

INHERITANCE

HD has a genetic component that predisposes an individual to the disease. Although no single direct cause has been determined, experts agree that a high correlation exists between certain genetic features and disease expression.

Genes are small regions of **DNA** found in all cell types of the body (including neurons) that contain instructions for cells to make small molecules called **proteins**. Proteins are required for the structure, function, and regulation of the body's cells, tissues, and organs. Each protein has unique functions. DNA is made up of smaller molecules called **bases** that are assembled together in a long chain. There are four possible bases (called A, T, C, and G) that, when read together like words in a recipe, encode different proteins. DNA is coiled up in structures known as chromosomes, of which humans have 23 pairs.

The gene associated with HD is located on chromosome number 4. This gene encodes a protein called **huntingtin**, which interacts with two proteins, found only in the brain, called huntingtin interacting protein (HIP1) and huntingtin-associated protein (HAP1). Because these proteins are located only in the brain, whereas huntingtin is located thought the entire body, HIP1 and HAP1 result in brain-specific effects.

An error in the sequence of bases results in an abnormal reading of their instructions and the creation of abnormal huntingtin protein. This malformed protein is stickier than the normal huntingtin protein and loops around and binds to itself, like a long strand of tape that has become tangled. So, rather than forming functional proteins, the abnormal huntingtin protein clumps up and forms protein aggregates that interfere with normal neuron functioning.

The error lies in a sequence of the gene composed of a series of repeating C-A-G bases. In normal individuals, this sequence contains about 20–30 C-A-G repeats, whereas in HD, the sequence is as long as 50 repeats, a significant increase in length. The number of C-A-G repeats in the huntingtin protein determines how it reacts with HIP1 and HAP1. Interestingly, a higher number of repeats is linked to an earlier onset of disease.

Each person has two copies of each chromosome, so there are two copies of all genes on each chromosome. So for the Huntington's disease gene on chromosome 4, individuals have two copies. Only one gene with excess C-A-G bases is needed for the increased expression of HD. This is called a **dominant allele**, and means that the children of one parent with HD have a 50% chance of inheriting the longer Huntingtin base sequence (see "Huntington's Disease Inheritance" box).

Huntington's Disease Inheritance

Huntington's disease is first evident around the age of 40, and results in death some 15 years later. The age of onset is thus well past the age at which people typically begin to start families. In the case of Huntington's, as well as with many other genetic disorders, the disease has not been removed by natural selection because the individual's genes have already been passed on through reproduction. The gene will not be "evolved out" because it offers no selective disadvantage until after reproduction, at which point—unfortunately—it is of no consequence to the genes.

Genetic testing is currently available to screen people with family histories of HD. These tests identify people who carry the HD gene and who are considered to be at risk for developing the disease. These results can be useful for people considering whether or not to begin a family and potentially pass the gene along to their children.

PATHOLOGICAL CHANGES

HD causes identifiable anatomical changes in the brain. Like people with Parkinson's disease, patients with HD exhibit degenerative changes within the basal ganglia, a cluster of midbrain nuclei that play a part in the control of muscle movements. In particular, the caudate and putamen structures (collectively known as the striatum) are involved in the planning and modulation of movement signals. The striatum also plays a role in cog-

Folk singer Woody Guthrie (1912–1967) had Huntington's disease. He inherited the disease from his mother, who died of HD when Woody was 15 years old. Two of Woody's children also had HD, although his singer-songwriter son, Arlo Guthrie, has apparently been spared.

nitive functions that involve planning, cognitive flexibility, abstract thinking, learning rules, and inhibiting inappropriate actions and irrelevant sensory information.

The striatum contains neurons that use a neurotransmitter called **GABA** (gamma-amino-butyric acid). So-called GABAergic neurons use GABA to transfer messages from one nerve to another, and because of their shape, are called spiny neurons. HD causes GABAergic neurons, as well as neurons that use **acetylcholine** as a neurotransmitter, to degenerate and to become reduced in density and activity. For some still unknown reason, these neurons are the first to die in HD. Under a microscope, it might appear that there are fewer neurons in the striatum, and scar-like formations of supporting **glia** become more prevalent. As a result of degeneration of striatum neurons, the dopamine neurons of the substantia nigra are also affected in such a way that they become overly active. For this reason, HD is often considered the opposite disorder from PD, in which the action of dopamine in the basal ganglia is reduced.

This degeneration and cell loss eventually results in a brain with a shrunken appearance. It is possible that the caudate and putamen **atrophy**, or shrink, decreasing to as much as 50% of their normal size, and the fluid-filled ventricles expand to occupy this empty space (termed *ex vacuo*) (Figure 3.2).

TREATMENT AND OUTLOOK

As of yet, no treatment or intervention can prevent the development, or stop the course, of HD. Drug regimens can help manage the behavioral symptoms such as chorea and depression. Most of the drugs used today act on the dopamine system that undergoes changes secondary to HD. Because degeneration of cells in the striatum causes unchecked dopamine action, drugs that block dopamine actions can ease symptoms associated with

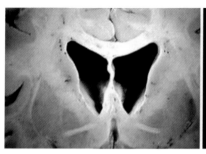 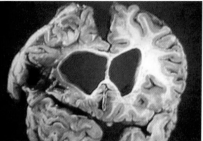

Figure 3.2 These photographs show the effect of HD on the basal gan-glia of the brain. The brain of the person with HD (*right*), compared with the normal brain (*left*), has larger ventricles, due to the death of nerve cells in that region.

chorea such as spasmodic movements of the limbs or face. Other drugs are used to treat depression, delusions, and other psychi-atric manifestations of HD.

■ **Learn more about Huntington's disease** Search the Internet for *dancing mania*, *black plague*, or *St. Vitus dance*.

4 Amyotrophic Lateral Sclerosis

One of the most important theoretical physicists of all time, Stephen Hawking, is an immobile captive, unable to move his body as a result of motor neuron disease. He has been confined to a wheelchair, unable to communicate except through a custom-made computer. Despite his illness, Hawking has made perhaps the most important contributions to our understanding of space and time since those of Albert Einstein. **Amyotrophic lateral sclerosis** (ALS), a disease that affects parts of the nervous system that control voluntary motor activity, is responsible for his impairment. This disease also affected baseball legend Lou Gehrig, and thus ALS is often referred to as "Lou Gehrig's disease."

Amyotrophic is a term used to describe a condition in which muscles of the body do not receive proper nourishment. Compounds required for muscle growth, energy storage, and repairs are obtained from the blood, whereas compounds that maintain connections between muscles and nerves are obtained through the nerves themselves. When the connection between a muscle and nerve is interrupted, the muscle does not receive the same signals and growth-related substances. Because our bodies prefer not to waste any excess energy, the muscles shrink and waste away. This is similar to the loss of muscle mass that results when people who once exercised regularly reduce their training or exercise. Historically, it was thought that muscle wasting away (atrophy) was the principal feature of ALS rather than a result of the disease, but we now know that because connections between muscles and nerves are damaged, muscle atrophy is secondary. *Lateral* is included in the name of the disease because the sides of the body affected by ALS are often asymmetrical, and *sclerosis* refers to hardened plaques observed in the spinal cords of people with ALS.

The **corticospinal tract** (CST) is a nerve pathway that originates in the brain within a region called the primary motor cortex (Figure 4.1). The motor cortex is a narrow band of brain cells at the top of the head that receives commands and input from nearly all other parts of the brain related to voluntary movement. Some neurons of the primary motor cortex are referred to as **upper motor neurons**, or **pyramidal cells**, based on their appearance. These cells are very large (presumably because of the large amounts of cellular machinery required to maintain a long axonal connection) and are found only in this area of the brain. Primary motor neurons send projections down into the brain stem and spinal cord to synapse, or connect, with second-order neurons. These second-order neurons, also referred to as **lower motor neurons**, act as the output cells of the nervous system. Their axons exit the spinal cord and wind across the body, down arms or legs, to connect to muscle fibers. Motor neurons send impulses to muscle groups through their axons that act like a wire, causing muscular contraction and relaxation.

ALS is associated with a progressive degeneration and the eventual loss of upper and lower motor neurons, and results in a decreased ability of these neurons to communicate with muscles. This, in turn, causes muscles to become weak and nonfunctional. People with ALS eventually become paralyzed. However, only voluntary muscular movements are impaired, and sensation is left intact. Cardiac and other muscle types are not susceptible to changes in ALS; therefore, patients with

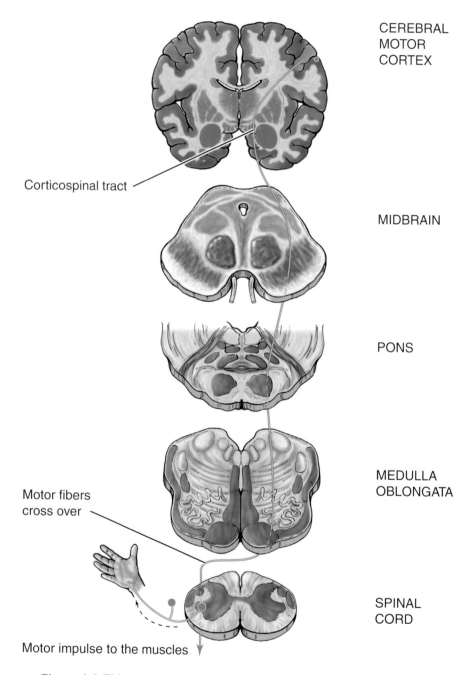

CEREBRAL
MOTOR
CORTEX

Corticospinal tract

MIDBRAIN

PONS

MEDULLA
OBLONGATA

Motor fibers
cross over

SPINAL
CORD

Motor impulse to the muscles

Figure 4.1 This diagram of the corticospinal tract shows how impulses move from the primary motor cortex to the muscle groups through this pathway.

advanced ALS are able to breathe on their own, maintain digestion, and have a normal heartbeat. This is because ALS affects only certain populations of neurons in the brain and spinal cord that are responsible for driving voluntary muscular movements. Neurons that drive the heart, diaphragm, and bowel, for example, are not damaged.

SIGNS AND SYMPTOMS

Symptoms of ALS may begin when people are in their late 40s to 50s. The medical literature nevertheless contains examples of individuals in their early 30s or at ages well beyond 50 who become sick. The question of why the disease takes so long to emerge is unanswered.

ALS begins with subtle deficiencies such as muscle weakness, clumsiness, or imprecise movements. Because upper and lower motor neurons are involved in both fine and gross control of movements, their degeneration can manifest as the inability to pick up a very small object or screw in a light bulb, or as suddenly falling over while walking. Sometimes, involuntary spasms of muscles in the arms or legs are noticed. The disease progresses to a point at which one side of the body experiences a greater degree of immobility, loss of intentional control, or complete paralysis, compared with the other side. Interestingly, the locations of symptoms spread to adjacent unaffected areas.

Upper and lower motor neurons perform somewhat different roles, and when either upper or lower motor neurons are damaged, different symptoms appear. With damage to only upper motor neurons, voluntary movements can still be performed. However, weakness, hyperreflexia (increased reflexes), and increased tightness are present. Damage to lower motor neurons is linked to weakness, fasciculation (involuntary contractions or twitching of a group of muscle fibers), and hyporeflexia (reduced reflexes) (Figure 4.2).

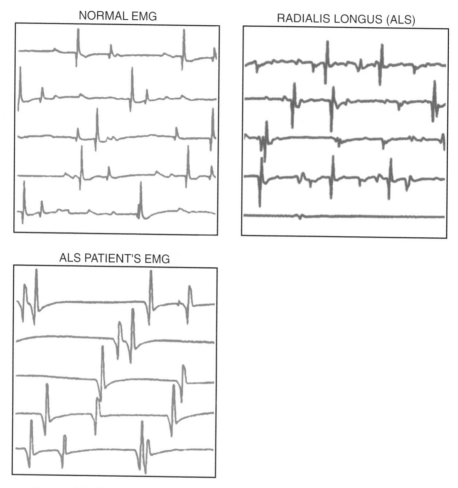

Figure 4.2 Electromyelogram (EMG) tracings show the speed of nerve conduction from normal individuals and from individuals with amyotropic lateral sclerosis (ALS). The differences between the tracings show that, in ALS patients, the height of the spikes is greater.

With ALS, the loss of motor neurons is not selective. Each population of neurons is equally susceptible to degeneration. Because of this, combinations of functional deficits are present;

for example, odd reflex responses are present (see "Babinski's Sign" box).

INHERITANCE

ALS can be genetically transmitted in families, but this is considered to be rare. The location of genetic mutation is on chromo-

Babinski's Sign

Damage to the corticospinal tract or incomplete *myelination* of the nervous system, as is the case with infants, produces Babinski's sign, an abnormal response in which the toes flare and the great toe moves in an upward direction when the sole of the foot is rubbed.

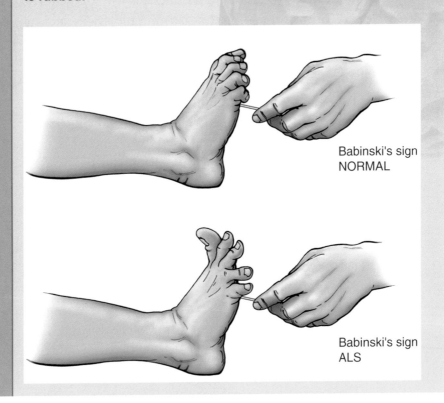

Babinski's sign
NORMAL

Babinski's sign
ALS

some 21, and only one copy of the defective gene is needed for the disease to be expressed (autosomal dominant). The mutation involves the gene coding for an enzyme called **superoxide dismutase** (SOD1).

SOD1 is involved in preventing damage to cells by harmful molecules called **free radicals**, atoms that have an odd number of electrons and are formed when oxygen reacts with certain molecules. Free radicals are very small molecules that can interact with a wide range of other molecules. These interactions are dangerous because they take place within critical cellular elements such as DNA or the cell's outer membrane, which, when damaged, almost certainly cause disruption of vital cellular processes and integrity. Once in action, free radicals can trigger cascading reactions that continue to damage cells, and possibly lead to cell death. SOD1 interacts with oxygen free radicals and converts them into less harmful molecules such as hydrogen peroxide, which are then converted to water and oxygen. This is the cell's first line of defense against free radicals. Consequently, in ALS, in which there is a mutation in the gene sequence with the instructions to make SOD1, the protective effects of SOD1 are reduced in the cells, allowing harmful free radicals to cause injury.

The other variety of ALS, called sporadic, is more common, but no definitive causes have been found. "Sporadic" means that the disease cannot be genetically linked to family members. A few theories have been advanced, however, that implicate **glutamate** as underlying the disease. Glutamate is an excitatory neurotransmitter. That is, when glutamate binds to a neuron, it makes it more likely to fire. The level of glutamate used by neurons to signal each other is highly sensitive. Too low a concentration of glutamate will lead to a lack of communication, whereas larger concentrations of glutamate cause higher-frequency firing rates. In either case, messages are imprecise. At a certain point, very high levels of glutamate cause neurons to fire so fast that they become damaged and eventually die. This process is called **excitotoxicity**. Tissues collected from the spinal cords of patients with ALS have shown them to be deficient in the ability to **reuptake** glutamate after it is released by neurons. An impaired ability to remove glutamate from neurons after release artificially creates a higher concentration of glutamate by permitting it to act for a longer time on receiving neurons. This results in high levels of stimulation and causes neurons to undergo excitotoxic death. Subsequent analysis of ALS spinal cords has shown that they have improperly functioning glutamate transporters, the molecules used by neurons to reuptake glutamate after release.

PATHOLOGICAL CHANGES

The most essential changes associated with ALS involve the degeneration and loss of motor neurons of the brain and spinal cord. In thinly sliced sections of the brain and spinal cord observed under a microscope, it is easy to see a reduced density of motor neurons. Some degree of scarring is also seen where neurons have been lost. In addition, the spinal cord itself becomes atrophied and shrunken, particularly in regions where motor-nerve roots emerge from the spinal cord.

TREATMENT AND OUTLOOK

No treatments are currently available to prevent or completely stop the progression of ALS. One drug, however, is approved by the FDA to extend the lives of those with ALS. This drug, called riluzole, inhibits the release of glutamate, and is associated with a reduction in the death of motor neurons caused by incomplete glutamate reuptake. Other drugs are being designed to interfere with glutamate synthesis, release, or binding to receptors.

Also in development are drugs that limit the formation of damaging free radicals. Recently, it has been suggested that natural antioxidants such as vitamin E, beta-carotene (a precursor to vitamin A), and vitamin C can reduce damage in ALS.

■ **Learn more about ALS** Search the Internet for *Lou Gehrig's disease, Stephen Hawking,* or *cosmology.*

5 | Seizure Disorders and Epilepsy

The experience of having a seizure can be simultaneously ecstatic and frightening. Depending on the type of seizure, patients report an initial sensation called an **aura**. The aura immediately precedes the seizure itself, and can often act as a forewarning that an episode is imminent. During this time, the person might experience strange sensations overtaking the body, such as warmth or a buzz, distinct smells such as ammonia or leather, visual hallucinations, or a wave of emotion. Some people with seizure disorders report feeling extreme highs, having a religious experience, or becoming "one with the universe." The New Testament (Acts 9:1–9:19) tells the story of a man called Saul who, on the way to the city of Damascus, was suddenly enveloped and blinded by a white light. He was struck off his feet, fell to the ground, and is said to have heard the voice of God. This report is consistent with the interpretation that Saul had experienced a seizure.

Seizures can be quite frightening, and can result in loss of consciousness, changes in breathing, muscle contractions, loss of bowel and bladder function, and forgetfulness. Often, individuals cannot remember or understand why they are lying on the ground, surrounded by a group of people.

Interestingly, in some cultures such as the Hmong community in Laos, illness is viewed as a disrupted link between body and soul. In one reported case, a young Hmong girl had epilepsy and her community attributed her condition to a wandering soul, referring to her seizures as her spirit catching her and making her fall down. This explanation, of course, stands in stark contrast to Western medicine's understanding of epilepsy.

In the United States, one in 100 people has experienced a seizure or been diagnosed with epilepsy. However, having a seizure does not necessarily mean that a person has epilepsy. A seizure can be caused by head trauma, high temperature, sickness, or reasons otherwise unidentified (see "Reflex Epilepsy" box). The distinction between a seizure disorder and epilepsy is often blurred. Generally, for a diagnosis of epilepsy to be made, a person must have had two or more seizure events.

The incidence of epilepsy is especially high in children and adolescents, perhaps because of a still developing brain where synaptic connections are being made and pruned, and where neurons are still undergoing organization along predetermined pathways. As the maturing brain becomes more stable, at around age 20, many people outgrow epilepsy. This form of epilepsy is called **benign childhood epilepsy.** Most children with generalized **tonic-clonic** and **partial seizures** have a "benign developmental disorder" that reduces their seizure threshold and is outgrown.

SIGNS AND SYMPTOMS

Seizure activity is essentially an uncontrolled electrical storm within the brain caused by misfiring groups of neurons. Typically, a neuron fires at 0–25 times/second when involved in signaling, but during a seizure, a neuron can fire at more than 60 times/second and propagate this signal to other neurons in its network. The local neuronal network then communicates the inappropriate bursting pattern to networks to which it is connected, and thus the seizure spreads.

The symptoms or types of seizures are determined by which areas of the brain are firing abnormally. For some reason, certain regions are more susceptible to seizure activity, perhaps because these areas have a higher sensitivity to input, greater

Reflex Epilepsy

Reflex epilepsy is a rare form of epileptic seizure triggered by external stimulation or sometimes even by specific types of thoughts or mental activity. The most common form is photosensitive epilepsy, where a seizure is induced by visual stimuli, such as bright flashes of light like those produced by a strobe light, leaves moving in sunlight, or video games like this one.

connectivity, or higher levels of ongoing signaling activity. For example, if a seizure begins in the frontal lobe (which is associated with higher thought processes, language, and planning motor activity), loss of consciousness and motor symptoms are most frequently observed. If the temporal lobe is involved, individuals experience a wide variety of symptoms because the temporal lobe is involved in sensation, emotional processing, memory formation, and recall. Because the parietal lobe is involved in bodily sensations, a seizure here can be manifested as changes in the sensory world. The occipital lobe is involved in visual processing, so seizure activity there results in visual hallucinations such as flashing lights or changes in color perception.

During a seizure, rapidly firing neurons undergo extreme metabolic demands. After these neurons turn off as they "tire out," the person may lose consciousness. It is not known if this is a natural response of the brain to shut down abnormal activity, or if the abnormal activity itself shuts down neurons.

The outward sign of epilepsy is the seizure (Figure 5.1). Currently, there are more than 40 types of seizures that are classified mainly based on whether or not there is a loss of consciousness. The two major categories are generalized and partial seizures, and under each of these categories are many other types of seizures. In some cases, partial seizures lead to generalized seizures as waves of activity pass over the entire brain.

Generalized seizures are defined by their ability to cause loss of consciousness and by rapid contraction of large numbers of muscles of the body. **Absence seizures** (formerly referred to as *petit mal*) cause the individual to become detached from reality for a short amount of time, sometimes with muscular contractions. During an absence seizure, the person may appear to be "spacing out" or staring off into space. **Tonic seizures** cause

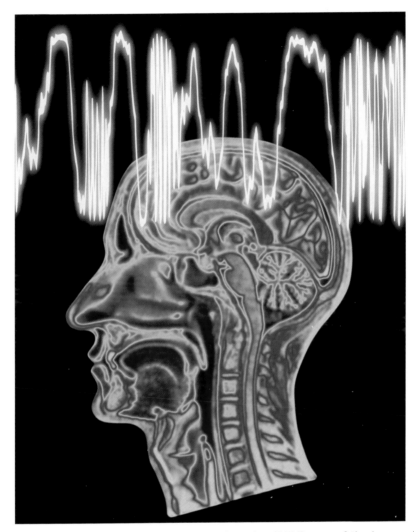

Figure 5.1 This colored magnetic resonance imaging (MRI) scan of the human brain shows a typical electroencephalogram (EEG) trace recorded during an epileptic seizure. The wave traces are irregular and chaotic during a seizure as unregulated electrical signals pass through the brain.

large muscle groups, such as those in the arms, legs, and back, to become rigid. There is no jerking or movement during a tonic seizure; the individual simply becomes rigid. **Clonic seizures** are characterized by rapidly jerking muscle contractions. A variation of clonic seizures is the **myoclonic seizure**, in which the individual experiences muscle contractions only in the upper body, arms, or legs. These are the most frequently observed muscle jerks associated with seizure. A combination seizure known as tonic-clonic also exists. Tonic-clonic activity is associated with a combination of effects: loss of consciousness, stiffening of the body, and falling, followed by jerking movements of the arms and legs. These seizures were formerly known as *grand mal* seizures. After a few minutes of activity, the body returns to rest, and consciousness returns. Finally, **atonic seizures** involve the sudden and temporary loss of voluntary muscle tone.

Partial seizures are perhaps more mysterious in their external appearance. Instead of causing a person to fall to the ground with jerky muscular contractions, partial seizures are more subtle and can affect sensory functions to a greater degree. For these reasons, partial seizures are often confused with psychosis, narcolepsy, and/or migraine headache, all of which can also be associated with changes in personality and dream-like states. In general, partial seizures occur in just one part of the brain. The consequences of **simple partial seizures** depend on the area of brain undergoing seizure activity. Typically, the individual remains conscious, but experiences strange sensations such as twitching, numbness, hearing or visual disturbances, feelings of déjà vu or familiarity, or sudden strong emotions, such as happiness, sadness, sickness, or elation. These things are often not noticeable to other people. **Complex partial seizures** result in a change or loss of consciousness, or entering into a trance, associated with smaller repetitive movements. Typically, these movements appear to be relatively normal in comparison with the jerking associated with generalized seizures. They include eye blinking, mouth movements such as lip pursing or repeated swallowing, throwing objects, or walking around in circles. Usually, partial seizures last only for several seconds, and are preceded by an aura that signals the imminent onset of a seizure (Figure 5.2).

INHERITANCE

Epilepsy has a genetic component. Family studies show that twins and siblings have a higher incidence of epilepsy than the normal population. This is supported by evidence that identical twins are more likely to share an epilepsy condition than non-identical twins. In many individuals, epilepsy is inherited as a single-gene trait, but in most cases, it is the result of highly complex genetic elements.

PATHOLOGICAL CHANGES

Seizures erupt from regions of the brain that have been found to be malformed. Structural abnormalities in the wiring or arrangement of neurons as a result of a birth defect often serve as a focus of seizure activity. Additionally, after a brain injury such as a penetrating wound or blow, scar tissue formation at or near the injury site can often lead to disruptions in the normal flow and communication of electrical impulses, giving rise to seizures. Abnormalities associated with blood vessels are often also **epileptogenic** (see "EEG and Traces" box).

For a long time, it has been known that **sodium channels** play a role in epilepsy. Sodium channels are proteins located on the outer membrane of neurons that open and close during firing, allowing sodium ions to enter the neuron and cause it to fire, termed *depolarization*. They are very important elements in neuronal firing and help determine the rate, length, and repriming

Figure 5.2 This artwork was done by a person with epilepsy to demonstrate the altered visual perception she experiences during a seizure.

characteristics of electrical discharges. Different channels can have different physiological characteristics, and can play different roles in the electrical properties of excitable cells. For example, abnormal alterations in sodium channel populations can enable neurons to reprime faster after firing, allowing the frequency of discharges to be higher and more repetitive than normal, making neurons **hyperexcitable**. This leads to abnormal burst-type firing and atypical network synchronization. For this

Figure 5.2 *(Continued)*

reason, drugs that specifically target sodium channels can effectively manage seizure disorders.

The seizure itself is generally thought not to produce great amounts of damage to the brain, although sometimes seizures that are excessive in duration or magnitude can damage structures. This conclusion is rather tenuous, however, because it is

EEG Tracing

An electroencephalograph (EEG) is commonly used to provide information regarding the electrical activity of the brain. During an EEG test, small electrodes are placed on the scalp to record waves of electrical activity of the brain through the skull. EEG tracings can identify generalized seizures, which usually show up as abnormal activity on both sides of the brain. In the case of partial epilepsy, however, abnormal activity may be observed in one or more areas of the brain.

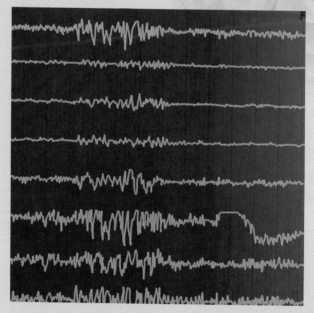

This EEG shows the electrical activity of the brain during a seizure.

often difficult to determine whether the damage was present before the onset of seizures and subsequent medical examination, or whether the seizures damaged the brain after the fact.

TREATMENT AND OUTLOOK

For most people diagnosed with epilepsy, successful management of the disease can be achieved primarily through drug therapy and, in some cases, surgery. In a small proportion of cases, seizures cannot be controlled, however.

Because sodium channels have been implicated as a cause of seizure disorders, a number of drugs that act on sodium channels have been developed specifically for the treatment of seizures. Sodium channel agents are the largest major class of antiepilepsy drugs. Sodium channels exist in three primary states: resting, open, and closed. Each of these states is associated with a different phase of the electrical current of the neuron, and the sum total of the time it takes to go through this cycle determines how fast a neuron can fire. When the channel is closed, the neuron is said to be **hyperpolarized**; when the channel is open, sodium ions can flow through the membrane and into the neuron. If this flow of sodium into the neuron is sufficient, and a threshold is met, the neuron fires (or **depolarizes**). The sodium channel then closes and no sodium ions can pass into the neuron; this state is known as **inactivation**. Inactivation is relieved by hyperpolarization, which resets the neuron to a resting rate where it is ready to depolarize again.

Sodium channel blocking drugs work by entering the inner pore of the sodium channel during its open state, and binding to a target site within the pore of the channel, effectively plugging it up. The result of this binding is to make the channels more inactive at lower membrane potentials, the electrical set-point of the neuron's membrane, and to delay the return of the channel to a resting, closed state. Both mechanisms prevent sustained firing of neurons at higher-than-normal rates, but do not affect normal firing rates. This prevents the generation and propagation of waves of excessive electrical activity from traveling across the cerebral cortex.

Surgical treatment of epilepsy is warranted in severe cases of seizure disorder. These procedures are meant to remove the part of the brain thought to serve as the focus of the hyperexcitability discharges, or to interrupt common pathways that propagate electrical discharges from one region of the brain to another. Removing a small **tumor** or abnormal growth of blood vessels is often all that is required to stop seizure activity. Cutting the **corpus callosum**, the thick fiber bundle that connects the two lateral hemispheres of the brain, is the only surgery available to stop generalized seizures. Selective removal of regions of the temporal lobe, including the hippocampus (a memory structure), work very well for easing temporal lobe epilepsy. Finally, multiple subpial transections, a technique that involves making shallow cuts in the outer surface of the brain, have been used to prevent the horizontal spread of abnormal neuronal activity across the cortex.

About 80% of patients who undergo epilepsy surgery experience a decrease in seizure activity. This benefit is offset, however, by the deficits caused by damaging the brain.

■ **Learn more about seizures and epilepsy** Search the Internet for *seizure art* or *cultural view of epilepsy.*

6 | Headache and Migraine

Headaches have been experienced by nearly everyone, and the familiar dull throbbing and aching can be quite uncomfortable and at times incapacitating. Many varieties of headache exist, each with different causes and symptoms. A headache is generally considered to be an irritation of the nerves around the face, head, neck, or inside of the skull or brain. However, as described below, headaches can take several different forms. Nerve irritation can be caused by muscular strain (for instance, holding the head in a downward position for too long), eye fatigue, dental or jaw problems, high blood pressure, hunger, and environmental or psychological stressors. Several classifications of headache exist, including tension, cluster, migraine, hormone, and secondary organic types (Figure 6.1). Migraines can be caused by the same stimuli as simple headaches, and often begin as headaches.

SIGNS AND SYMPTOMS

The most common form of headache is the **tension headache**. This type of headache is nonspecific, meaning that the cause is not related to any identifiable factor. The cause of tension headaches is probably neurochemical imbalances within the brain, and/or muscle tensing at the back of the neck, face, or scalp. Muscles can become tight as a result of stressful situations, anxiety, overuse, or prolonged activity. Pain asso-

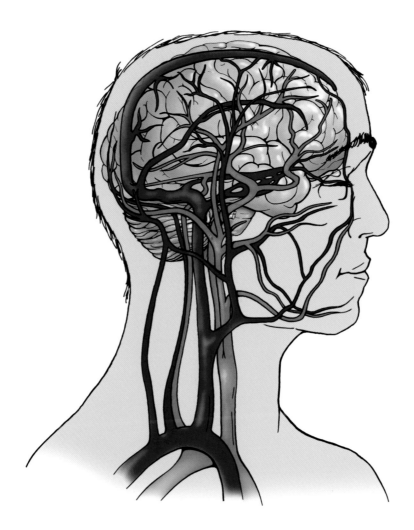

Figure 6.1 Nearly everybody will experience a headache at some time. There are many varieties of headaches, each with different causes and symptoms.

ciated with tension headaches is generally restricted to the outside of the head, often described as band-like and symmetrical. Tension headaches can be classified depending on how often they occur: episodic (around one per month), frequent (every few days), or chronic (every other day). Typically, frequent and

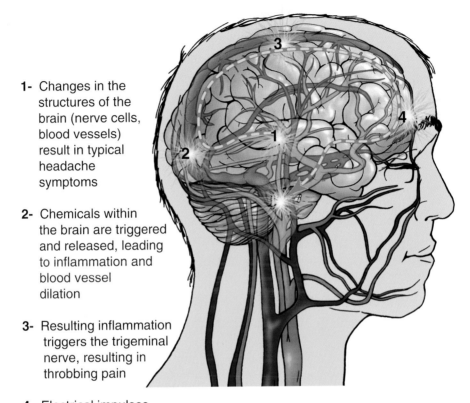

1- Changes in the structures of the brain (nerve cells, blood vessels) result in typical headache symptoms

2- Chemicals within the brain are triggered and released, leading to inflammation and blood vessel dilation

3- Resulting inflammation triggers the trigeminal nerve, resulting in throbbing pain

4- Electrical impulses spread to other regions of the brain

Figure 6.2 Changes within the interactions between nerves and blood vessels lead to migraine headaches.

chronic forms evolve from episodic types, and may coexist with migraine. Chronic tension headaches often interfere with daily activities by impairing concentration, causing insomnia, and producing nausea.

Migraine headaches (Figure 6.2) are the more severe forms of headache, affecting 28 million Americans. They usually occur on one side of the head only, and are characterized by sharp, throbbing pains. They are often associated with nausea, vomiting, and sensitivity to light and sound. Migraine headaches are so severe that they can disrupt everyday tasks. Often the migraine sufferer must be in a completely dark and quiet room because even the slightest stimulation can make the headache more severe. Migraines can last up to several hours, and follow a similar pattern of progression from pre-headache to headache to post-headache.

During the pre-headache phase, an aura may be experienced for a short time before the headache begins. The aura is typically visual, and can take the form of bright flashing lights or spots, zigzag lines, wavy images, or shimmering around the edges of objects referred to as a scintillating scotoma (dazzling blind spots). Dizziness and ringing in the ears are sometimes also experienced.

Migraines are often triggered by internal or external events that vary among individuals. These include events from the environment (such as odors, loud sounds, or change in altitude), diet (foods such as cheese and red wine, or low blood sugar), intense physical activity, emotional stress, and hormones. Regardless of whether the stimulus is from inside or outside of the body, the final result is that migraines emerge from inflammatory processes taking place inside the brain.

The vascular theory of migraine headache was proposed in the 1940s. This theory suggests that abnormalities in blood flow are the cause of migraines. Constriction of blood vessels within the brain is followed by dilation of blood vessels that results in activation of pain-sensing nerves within the vessel walls. This theory has become outdated because we now know that the changes in vascular tone observed in migraine are not sufficient to produce symptoms.

Serotonin (5-hydroxytryptamine, 5-HT), a neurotransmitter found in the brain, has recently been implicated in causing migraines. Several lines of evidence support this theory: 1) increased levels of 5-HT in blood and urine are found at different phases of migraine, 2) drugs that increase the release of 5-HT can cause migraines, and 3) inhibition of a class of 5-HT receptors constricts blood vessels (dilated blood vessels cause decreased blood flow) and decreases migraine intensity. The 5-HT hypothesis represents a refinement of the classic vascular theory.

Regardless of the underlying mechanisms, migraine pain results directly from the interaction of the **trigeminal nerve** and blood vessels that surround the brain. The trigeminal nerve emerges from the base of the brain and fans out across the face and jaw. It is responsible for muscular activity of the eyes, face, mouth, and jaw, and sensory functions relayed from the face to the brain. Branches of the trigeminal nerve that innervate the teeth are silenced with drugs during dental procedures. Pain signals are sent to the brain by the trigeminal nerve from blood vessels at its base. Once received by the brain, high-intensity pain information serves to feed forward on itself, further exaggerating the intensity and causing high-frequency firing of neurons that convey information regarding pain. Because the nervous system encodes the intensity of a stimulus by rate of firing, the brain interprets this firing as a higher and higher degree of pain.

Cluster headaches (also known as histamine headaches) are perhaps the least common form of headache, affecting only 1% of the population. The term *cluster* is used to describe the grouped sequence of instances that occur from weeks to months at a time and then spontaneously end. The frequency of attacks is higher in the fall or spring, but the connection to allergies is not clear (higher amounts of rain result in mold during fall and pollen increases during the spring, causing a sudden release of histamines or serotonin). As with migraine, cluster headache pain is linked to interactions between the trigeminal nerve and blood vessels surrounding the brain. Additionally, because of their often repetitive time of onset during the day, cluster headaches have been linked to the **hypothalamus**, a structure deep in the brain that controls basic physiological processes such as body rhythms and temperature.

Symptoms of a cluster headache typically occur on one side of the head. Sudden sharp pain is usually experienced behind the eye, and radiates outward across the forehead, temple, or cheek of the same side. Swelling around the eye, tearing, runny nose, or congestion may also be present. For some reason, headaches occur frequently during sleep.

A large number of women have linked their monthly menstrual cycle to the occurrence of headaches. Some women have severe headaches at specific times in their cycle, which correspond to increasing and decreasing levels of the female hormones estrogen and progesterone that regulate the cycle. These **hormone headaches** are also associated with other events linked to sex hormones, including pregnancy, use of birth control pills, menopause, and hormone replacement therapy.

Secondary headaches are experienced as symptoms originating with other diseases or disorders. For example, a tumor of the brain might apply pressure on a blood vessel or the trigeminal nerve and result in headache. Infection of the covering surrounding the brain or high blood pressure can also put pressure on the trigeminal nerve. Aneurysms and problems with the eye, ear, and nose, can cause headaches. These headaches are often associated with other neurological problems, such as weakness of a part of the body, seizure, memory changes, vomiting, loss of consciousness, and so forth. Approximately 50% of patients with brain tumors experience headaches that resemble tension or migraine types.

INHERITANCE

Migraines have a genetic component. A high percentage of migraine sufferers have a family history of migraines. A child has a 75% chance of developing migraine if both parents have migraine and 50% if only one parent is positive. The mode of inheritance of migraine is quite complicated, and no single gene has been identified that predisposes an individual to migraine. Rather, the heritability appears to have many factors.

PATHOLOGICAL CHANGES

Headaches very rarely cause damage to the brain or surrounding structures, and typically no structural abnormalities can be seen with brain imaging techniques. Sometimes, however, these problems can be detected in the case of secondary headaches cause by tumors, abnormalities with blood vessels, or injury.

TREATMENT AND OUTLOOK

Typically, non-migraine headaches, such as tension headaches, can be treated with over-the-counter painkillers such as acetaminophen, ibuprofen, or aspirin. These drugs are antiinflammatory drugs and reduce tissue swelling. Often, antidepression drugs are used for tension headaches. These compounds act on the 5-HT system and are effective in reducing headache pain.

Treatment of cluster headaches is a bit more complicated. It aims both to reduce the pain associated with headache and to shorten the duration of the cluster time. Drugs used to alleviate cluster headaches are similar to those used for migraine.

Management of migraine headaches is also complicated and involves both preventative and abortive treatments. Preventative treatments are designed to reduce the number of migraines a person experiences, while abortive treatments are designed to ease the symptoms and shorten the duration of a migraine attack once it has begun. With migraines, it is important to begin treatment as soon as possible because as the pain signals become stronger over time and sensitize brain pain-processing circuitry, headaches may grow even more intense.

Drugs commonly used to prevent migraines include 5-HT agents, antidepressants, anticonvulsants, beta-blockers, calcium-channel blockers, and ergot derivatives. Selective 5-HT reuptake inhibitors, drugs that prolong the action of 5-HT at specific sites in the brain, are widely used. Recall that as the migraine progresses, levels of 5-HT decrease, and blood vessels within the brain dilate. As the migraine subsides, levels of 5-HT also return. Stimulating a particular class of 5-HT receptors by slowing recycling 5-HT into the cell after release can improve symptoms and speed recovery during migraine by causing vasoconstriction and reducing inflammation of blood vessels. The drawback of 5-HT agents is that they may not exert their effects until after several weeks of treatment. An older class of 5-HT reuptake inhibitors called tricyclic antidepressants also blocks 5-HT reabsorption into neurons after it is released during signaling, but tends to produce more severe side effects.

Antiseizure drugs commonly used for treating epilepsy are also effective in treating migraine. The exact mechanism of their action is not known, but they are thought to help limit changes in blood vessel tone.

Beta-blockers are the most widely used preventative drugs. They block the effects of substances that are normally present, such as epinephrine (adrenaline), that excite the heart and blood vessels. Beta-blockers reduce these effects, acting on the heart and blood vessels to cause vascular contraction. Interactions have also been established for beta-blockers and the 5-HT system.

Calcium-channel blockers act on small pores of thin muscles that wrap around blood vessels and allow entry of calcium ions into the cell. Entry of calcium is associated with lowered blood pressure, reduced heart contraction force, and dilation of arteries. Calcium-channel blockers inhibit artery dilation and block the release of 5-HT, producing relief from migraine.

Abortive migraine treatments are similar to those used to suppress non-migraine headaches, and include over-the-counter pain antiinflammatory drugs. In cases of migraines that are unresponsive to traditional drugs, ergot alkaloids are often used. Ergot derivatives were originally isolated from plants such as belladonna (so named because of its historical use as a cosmetic by Italian women to dilate the pupils). These compounds stimulate 5-HT release and reverse blood vessel dilation around the brain.

■ **Learn more about headache and migraine** Search the Internet for *scintillating scotoma* or *aura experience*.

7 Stroke

A stroke is similar in many ways to a heart attack, in which the flow of blood to the heart muscle is interrupted. A stroke can be thought of as a brain attack in which a portion of the brain is starved of blood for either a short or long period of time. The brain must receive oxygen through a constant supply of blood because it cannot store oxygen on its own. Because blood carries oxygen and nutrients necessary for proper functioning of brain cells, any interruption of this vital supply can cause devastating effects. After an interruption of blood flow for only three to four minutes, neurons start to die.

Stroke is the third most common cause of death and the leading cause of major disability in the United States, affecting as many as 3.8 million people a year.

TYPES OF STROKE

The two major types of stroke, hemorrhagic and ischemic, differ remarkably in their nature. **Hemorrhagic stroke**, the more serious of the two types, occurs when a weakened blood vessel within the brain suddenly ruptures. This burst causes blood to pour from the opened vessel. High blood pressure is the major cause of hemorrhagic stroke, responsible for 65% of all strokes. High blood pressure causes the heart and blood to put increased pressure on the walls of blood vessels. This can weaken the vessels and set them up for a failure. High blood pressure also increases the deposition of fatty plaques (arteriosclerotic, see below) on the inner walls of vessels; these deposits can break off and cause **ischemic stroke**.

Ischemic stroke results from closing off of (termed *occlusion*), or low flow in, one or more blood vessels in the brain. This occurs when a clot develops and cuts off blood supply. A number of different types of clots have been classified, including a **thrombus**, a blood clot that forms in the brain, and an **embolus**, a blood clot that forms in another part of the body (such as the neck, lungs, or lining of the heart) and travels into the brain. One way an embolus forms is through a type of irregular heartbeat called atrial fibrillation in which the heart's normal pumping rhythm is disrupted and small clots can form as blood remains in small eddies within the heart. **Arteriosclerotic clots** are formations of fatty deposits around the inner walls of blood vessels that break off.

A **transient ischemic attack** can happen when blood flow to a certain region of the brain is interrupted briefly. After this interruption, normal blood flow is generally restored on its own.

The brain receives blood through two main supply sources: the **carotid artery** and **basilar artery**. These vessels supply the entire brain. The carotids comprise the major source of cerebral circulation. The carotid arteries come from the heart and travel up the front of the neck on both sides; this is the pulse you can feel when you place your fingertips on either side of the trachea (windpipe) underneath the jaw. The basilar artery is located at the base of the skull and travels on the underside of the brain. These main arteries supply the front and rear portions of the brain, but each divides and branches off into smaller vessels at a number of points, to supply more local regions of brain tissue.

Together, the carotids branch into the anterior and middle cerebral arteries that supply the front (anterior) portion of the brain. If there is an obstruction in a carotid or its branches, deficits in motor and sensory function are observed. Language deficits are also observed in strokes that involve the anterior circulation. Ischemic strokes occurring in the anterior circulation are the most common of all ischemic strokes, accounting for approximately 70% of all cases. Ischemic stroke accounts for more than 80% of all strokes. The basilar artery branches to form the posterior cerebral arteries, which supply blood to the back part of the hemispheres, brain stem, and cerebellum. Occlusion of the basilar artery or its branches results in loss of vision, vertigo, and changes in balance and coordination.

Another area susceptible to strokes is referred to as collateral circulation. The anterior communicating artery connects the two anterior cerebral arteries, and the posterior communicating arteries connect each carotid artery to the basilar artery. This system of collaterals forms a structure called the Circle of Willis. The purpose of the Circle of Willis is to distribute the incoming blood flow throughout the brain, especially in the case of injury to one or more of the major vessels. Because the brain is so sensitive to even a brief interruption of blood flow, this is a very important structure (loss of consciousness results after just 10 seconds of interrupted blood flow, and after 3–4 minutes of no flow neurons begin to die). Should either of the carotids or basilar artery become occluded or cut, the Circle of Willis will permit the continued flow of blood downstream of the insult. In fact, just one intact carotid could supply the entire brain with blood because of the distribution arrangement of the Circle of Willis (Figure 7.1).

The area of stroke damage in the brain can be large or small, depending on the size of a thrombus. For example, if a large clot that forms in the lungs is ejected through the heart and into the carotids or basilar arteries, it can occlude one of these major feeders and result in widespread damage. On the other hand, if a clot is small and passes through the large vessels to become lodged in smaller downstream vessels, the region of brain damage will be smaller.

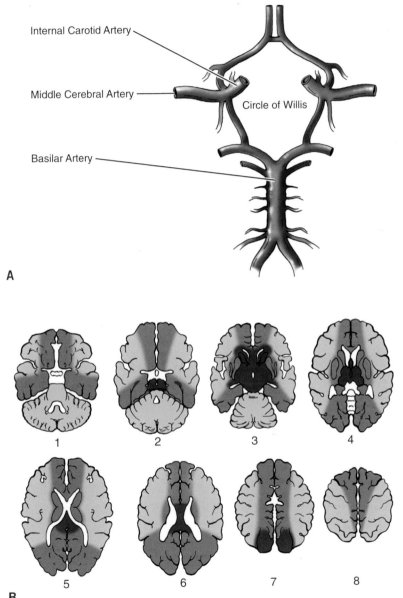

Internal Carotid Artery

Middle Cerebral Artery

Basilar Artery

Circle of Willis

A

1   2   3   4

5   6   7   8

B
Figure 7.1 Located at the base of the brain, the Circle of Willis **(A)** permits blood to flow throughout the brain even if the supply from one of the major vessels is disrupted. It receives blood directly from the heart and distributes it throughout the brain **(B)** as shown here.

SIGNS AND SYMPTOMS

Having a stroke can be quite a strange experience, and the results of a stroke can change the course of a person's life. Almost instantaneously, the person suffering a stroke can undergo changes in how the body functions. Sometimes these changes are very slight, while other times they can be quite dramatic. A typical experience is one in which the person wakes up in the middle of the night to use the bathroom and finds an entire side of the body immobile (termed hemiparesis, a Latin word meaning one-sided weakness). The person typically describes this feeling as being "frozen," "dead," or "too heavy to move." In such situations, people often decide that the cause of this feeling is the position in which they slept, so they return to bed, only to find that the impairment still exists when they wake up in the morning. Typically, the symptoms of a stroke are worse initially, but they can sometimes shift and change subtly in the time following the attack. Hemiparesis shows itself as muscle weakness that may be present with abnormal stiffness or spasticity. When standing, the person's affected leg may suddenly become unstable and buckle. This will make walking difficult and may cause the person to suddenly fall over. Because one side of the body is not controllable, balance in general is disturbed (Figure 7.2).

Hemiparesis is just one of several signs of a stroke. Sudden weakness of other parts of the body can be present, including the face, or a single arm or leg, but these symptoms are typically restricted to one side of the body. A sudden paralysis of the arm, leg, and trunk on the same side of the body, called **hemiplegia**, is often present. If the stroke affects the part of the brain responsible for language comprehension or speech production, the person will be unable to understand words or speak. This condition is known as aphasia. Broca's aphasia refers to the inability to produce speech, while Wernicke's aphasia is the inability to understand speech. Similarly, if the stroke affects the visual centers of the brain, a person may experience a sudden

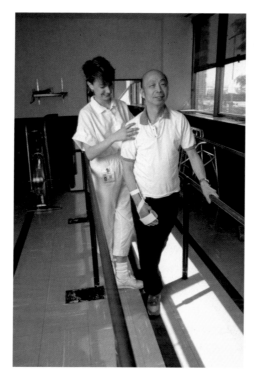

Figure 7.2 This photo shows a patient with hemiparesis, a weakening or paralysis of one side of the body, that sometimes follows a stroke.

blurring of vision or deficits in one or both eyes. In many cases, stroke causes a sudden intense headache.

These symptoms indicate which region of the brain has suffered an interruption of blood flow during a stroke, and provide valuable clues to doctors treating the patient. Recall that the brain is organized into distinct regions that perform specific tasks, or send and receive signals from different parts of the body. Thus, the effects of a stroke are determined by the extent and location of brain damage.

INHERITANCE

There seems to be a minor genetic risk for stroke; however, the genetic factors associated with stroke are difficult to determine because of its many environmental causes. It is known, however, that genetic susceptibility to increased blood pressure or stress may account for a significant degree of the inheritance of ischemic stroke.

Genetically weak vessel walls may be one cause of stroke. Blood vessels are made up of several layers of connective tissue, muscle, and other materials that enable them to accommodate the high pressure of blood. For example, if a genetic alteration is responsible for flawed collagen, a structural element, vessel walls will be weaker and susceptible to rupture. One example is Marfan's syndrome, in which the structural integrity of vessels is impaired and patients are at risk for hemorrhagic stroke.

High blood pressure, elevated cholesterol levels, heart disease, smoking, and being overweight all significantly increase the risk of stroke.

PATHOLOGICAL CHANGES

The outcome of stroke is quite simple—death of neurons. Stroke results in an immediate central area of damage called an **ischemic core**, and a surrounding area called the **ischemic penumbra**. Because neurons die within a few minutes of interrupted blood flow, a great deal of neuron loss occurs at the core of a stroke's territory. A cascade of events takes place within neurons at the ischemic core: 1) reductions in blood flow cause excitatory amino acids such as glutamate to be released in high concentrations, which can kill neurons by causing them to fire at very high rates; 2) glutamate opens up channels in neuronal membranes that allow other substances such as calcium into the cells, which release additional harmful substances toxic to cells; and 3) free radicals that play a role in neuronal damage are released.

In the penumbra around the ischemic core, tissue may be supplied by other sources of blood in addition to the primary source (now blocked), where the flow is not completely interrupted. These regions are said to be "hypoperfused" and receive just enough blood to remain alive. However, if prolonged, this oxygen starvation will eventually result in cell death. Thus, one of the main goals of stroke treatment is restoring blood flow to the ischemic penumbra. If this can be done rapidly after ischemia, injured neurons can possibly recover and patients may achieve some gain in function.

There are some other experimental compounds that target the secondary cascade of injury in the penumbra region following stroke. After an ischemic period, neurons and other brain cells begin to undergo different types of death, depending on how close they are to the injury site. Neurons receiving blood supply directly from the stroke site are almost certainly destined for death, whereas neurons in immediately adjacent penumbra are less likely to die. Neurons in the penumbra carry out a type of suicide that involves the activation of a number of genes, proteins, and biochemical cascades that can be interrupted. It is hoped that agents targeting this death process can rescue neurons in this zone from death.

TREATMENT AND OUTLOOK

Currently, only ischemic strokes can be treated with drugs, and the window of therapeutic opportunity is very brief (within three hours). During an ischemic stroke in which a blood clot has formed and lodged within a blood vessel, certain chemicals called **thrombolytic** drugs are administered into the blood (Figure 7.3). These drugs decrease the blood's ability to clot and also break up recently formed clots. One such drug, called tissue plasminogen activator, rapidly dissolves the blood clots that cause many strokes, thereby restoring blood flow, salvaging ischemic brain tissue, and reducing the amount of damage that strokes produce.

Remarkably, the brain is able to repair itself to some degree after stroke. Over the course of weeks or months, recovery of some functions is not uncommon in some patients. In these cases, through the ability to reorganize intact circuitry, the brain can learn to compensate for lost functions through training and

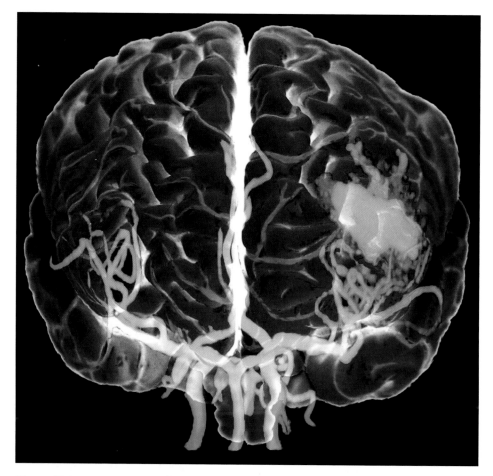

Figure 7.3 This colored three-dimensional magnetic resonance angiography (MRA) scan of a stroke victim's brain shows internal bleeding (pink, center right). The brain damage of a stroke results from pressure from the internal bleeding. The brain is seen from the front. The bleeding is in the left hemisphere of the brain, and has caused hemiplegia in the right half of the body.

physical therapy. Remodeling of the cerebral cortex takes place by recruiting adjacent cortical areas to do tasks in which they were previously only partially involved, or by creating new circuits and connections to replace damaged ones (Figure 7.4).

■ **Learn more about stroke** Search the Internet for *cortical plasticity* or *stroke and relearning.*

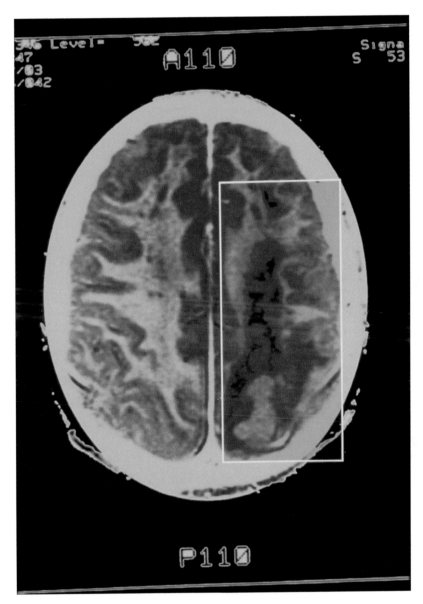

Figure 7.4 False-color CT scan of a cross section of the head showing a region of the brain (boxed) where a blood vessel has ruptured, resulting in intracerebral hemorrhage (dark red and black areas).

8 | Brain Tumors

A **tumor** is an abnormal collection of cells that grows spontaneously and multiplies uncontrollably. Brain tumors most often occur in people over the age of 45. In the United States, approximately 17,000 new cases of cancerous primary brain tumors occur yearly, and 13,300 people die because of them. Primary or metastatic tumors develop in about 35,000 adult Americans. In children, in whom the brain is developing, brain tumors are the second leading cancer-related cause of death.

TYPES OF BRAIN TUMORS

Tumors are described as being either benign or malignant, based on their rates of growth and ability to spread (Figure 8.1). **Benign tumors** are noncancerous and do not spread to other parts of the brain. They grow very slowly, but irrespective of their rates of proliferation, benign tumors are still quite dangerous. Because of their slow-growing nature, they are easier to localize and remove. After removal, benign tumors are not likely to recur. **Malignant tumors** are cancerous tumors that migrate to other parts of the brain. Their rate of growth is high, as is their tendency to invade other healthy tissue. Because of their aggressive qualities and likeliness to destroy nearby tissue, malignant tumors are life-threatening.

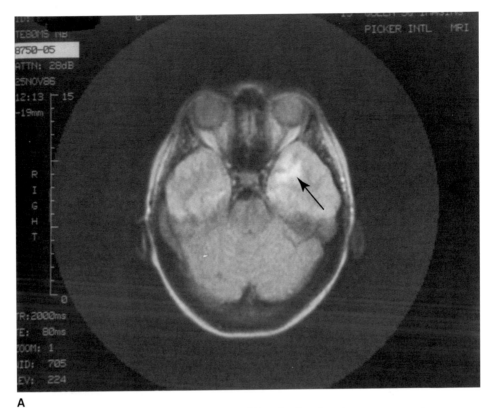

A

Figure 8.1 **(A)** Brain tumors can either be benign (noncancerous), as seen here (*arrow*) behind the eye on the right side of the brain as a bright white spot, or malignant (cancerous). Benign tumors are easier to remove, but both types of tumors are extremely dangerous.

Even the smallest brain tumor can quickly produce damage. Unlike tumors of the body that can grow unchecked for quite some time because they can displace other organs or tissues, brain tumors exist within the confines of the skull and immediately compress nearby structures and tissue. Remember that the skull is a closed space, so there is no room for the brain to grow.

Brain tumors are typically classified as primary or secondary, depending on their place of origin. **Primary tumors** are made up of cells of the same type of tissue in which the tumor forms. As such, a primary brain tumor originates from the cells of the brain. This type of tumor is further classified according to the

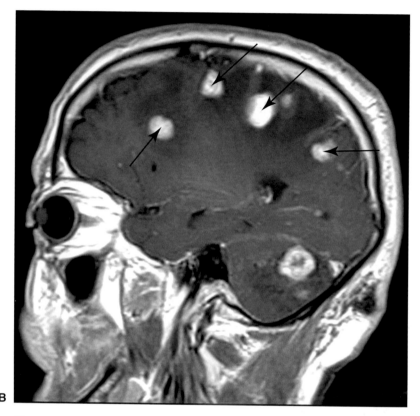

Figure 8.1 *(Continued)* **(B)** MRI of a brain showing multiple malignant tumors, which appear as white spots on the gray background of the brain *(arrows)*.

type of cell from which the tumor is formed, or from the cell type from which the tumor originated. Recall that the brain is made up of neurons and a number of supportive cell types that act as structural elements, supply cells with nutrients, or are part of the **immune system.**

Tumors call **gliomas** can form from glial cells, a type of cell in the brain that provides structural support to brain tissue and performs a number of metabolic functions necessary for the biochemical support of neurons. Several different types of gliomas exist, including the cancerous **astrocytomas** and the less common and usually benign **oligodendrogliomas**. Astrocytes, the largest and most numerous glial cells in the brain and spinal cord, are star-shaped cells that connect to a number of neurons and regulate the chemical environment surrounding both neurons and glia. Astrocytes are present everywhere in the brain, especially in areas of high neuron density, such as the frontal and temporal lobes.

Astrocytomas are tumors that form from astrocytes. Approximately 25% of all brain tumors are astrocytomas. Many astrocytoma subtypes exist based on their appearance when seen through a microscope and their rate of growth or aggressiveness. One form that can be potentially highly aggressive in its growth is called a **glioblastoma multiforme**. Such astrocytomas are the most common primary brain tumors in adults. Because the rapid growth of this type of tumor compresses or destroys normal healthy brain tissue, it can spread into nearby brain structures and tissues and cause a significant degree of swelling and tissue destruction.

Oligodendrocytes, glial cells that are shaped much like astrocytes, have slender processes and fewer branches. Oligodendrocytes are found in close proximity to neurons and serve to electrically insulate axons by wrapping them with many layers of a fatty substance called **myelin**. The myelin acts like insulation around a wire, and its disruption makes axons unable to conduct messages properly. Oligodendrogliomas make up fewer than 5% of all brain tumors and are less harmful than other tumor types. They grow very slowly, and typically are benign. Occasionally, a tumor can be made up of a mixture of astrocytes and oligodendrocytes. This unique type of tumor is called an **oligoastrocytoma**.

Tumors can also form in the protective tissue layers that surround the brain called the meninges. **Meningiomas** are typically benign and slow growing, but although they are not found directly within the brain itself, they can still cause many problems. Overgrowth of cells in this area can compress healthy brain tissue and cause neurological dysfunction. For unknown reasons, meningiomas occur more frequently in women than in men.

The pituitary gland is a small structure at the base of the brain, behind the nose, that secretes hormones that control and regulate growth and metabolism. The pituitary is divided into two parts, each of which secretes different hormones. The anterior (front) portion of the pituitary secretes growth hormone, prolactin (which stimulates milk production), adrenocorticotrophic hormone (which stimulates the adrenal glands), thyroid-stimulating hormone (which stimulates the thyroid), follicle-stimulating hormone (which stimulates the testes and ovaries). The posterior (back) pituitary secretes antidiuretic hormone (which controls water retention) and oxytocin (which drives uterine contractions during childbirth, and breast milk production). **Pituitary adenomas** are tumors of the pituitary gland, most of which are benign and noncancerous. They are referred to as *adenomas* because they are tumors of glandular origin. Pituitary tumors exist as either secreting or nonsecreting; secreting tumors produce and release higher than normal amounts of pituitary hormones into the blood. In these cases, the brain tumor affects the entire body. In the brain, the tumor may cause loss of vision because a pituitary overgrowth can compress nearby optic nerves that transmit signals from the eyes to the brain. Pituitary tumors sometimes produce excess amounts of growth hormone that lead to **gigantism**.

Tumors of cells that line the inner surfaces of fluid-filled compartments of the brain are called epenymomas. These types of tumors are rare. **Ependymomas** cause the overproduction of cerebrospinal fluid and result in compression of brain structures.

Brain tumors do not necessarily originate in the brain, but can start in other parts of the body and spread to the brain. These so-called **secondary tumors** are made up of cancer cells that have **metastasized**, or traveled, through the blood to the brain, where they begin to grow. Typical sources include the lungs, breast, and digestive tract. These types of brain tumor are much more common than primary tumors. Most metastatic brain tumors are found widely distributed through the brain rather than localized in a single area. Therefore, these tumors are difficult to treat, and the probability of a favorable recovery is low.

SIGNS AND SYMPTOMS

Symptoms of a brain tumor, like those of stroke, provide evidence of where the tumor has formed. Both size and location of a tumor give clues to its type. Tumor expansion within the brain causes two types of symptoms: increased pressure within the head, and disruption of brain function. Increased pressure is caused by the growing mass of cells, by the swelling associated with metastatic tumors, by an increase in the production of cerebrospinal fluid, or by blockage of its flow. Tumors at the back of the brain within the occipital lobe, which is involved in visual processing, often result in visual abnormalities. Tumors within the temporal lobe result in loss of hearing. Symptoms may also provide clues about the type of tumor cells. For example, because of their involvement with the electrical firing of neurons, astrocytomas frequently cause seizures.

Other general symptoms of brain tumors involve a different or unfamiliar form of headache, memory problems, nausea, numbness or tingling in parts of the body, changes in balance and hearing, and seizures. Because the cortex of the brain is organized so that the entire body is laid out on the surface, particular sensory or motor disturbances can provide valuable clues to tumor location. If a tumor is located in a motor region that controls arm or leg movement, the person will show signs of difficulty (on the opposite side of the body) corresponding to the body part that the damaged area of the brain controls. With tumors that affect sensory areas of the brain, an individual might experience numbness, pain, or tingling in a body part associated with the damaged brain region.

With slower-growing tumors, the brain can sometimes accommodate the growth of the tumor and signs are not noticeable for some time. On the other hand, with tumors that grow at faster, symptoms may be noticed much sooner because the brain has no time to accommodate the change.

INHERITANCE AND CAUSES

The familial incidence of cancer is approximately 15% in people with brain tumors. However, it is not known whether a predisposition to cancers also makes brain cells susceptible to tumor formation, or if cancers simply metastasize to the brain (see "Cell Phones and Brain Tumors" box).

Evidence also points to chromosomal and genetic abnormalities in patients with brain tumors. Certain diseases that have a genetic component cause tumors to grow on nerve tissue. For example, neurofibromatosis produces skin and bone abnormalities and causes tumors of the nerves involved in hearing called acoustic neuromas, as well as meningiomas and gliomas. Chromosomal abnormalities include an abnormally high number of copies or deletions of chromosome 7 or 22. It is likely that these chromosomes are the location of tumor-suppressing genes, which, if disrupted, can lead to extensive tumor growth. In the case of extra copies of chromosomes, it is possible that these chromosomes contain genes that promote cancer.

PATHOLOGICAL CHANGES

Brain tumors are relatively straightforward in their appearance and pathology, and most are easily detectable by medical imaging techniques such as **computerized tomography** (CT) and **magnetic resonance imaging** (MRI) (Figure 8.2). With these two-dimensional pictures of the brain, the tumor can be easily localized and its borders described. Because brain tumors are made of the same type of soft tissue and are located in other soft tissues, MRI scans are particularly useful in identifying brain tumors. New imaging techniques allow for three-dimensional reconstruction of tumors in a model of the patient's brain. These images can be moved around in the computer, and used in the operating room to localize tumors.

TREATMENT AND OUTLOOK

The typical course of treatment for a brain tumor uses a combination of surgery, radiation, and chemotherapy to stop growth

(*continued on page 79*)

Cell Phones and Brain Tumors

Recently, the use of cellular telephones has been accused of contributing to the incidence of brain tumors. The theory is that electromagnetic radiation emitted by cellular telephones placed in close proximity to the brain might cause abnormal cell growth through mutations in DNA. A number of clinical studies involving more than 3,000 patients produced findings that were either inconclusive or showed no indication of higher brain tumor risk among persons who had used handheld cellular phones compared to those who had not used them. More importantly, there was no evidence of increasing risk with increasing years of use or average minutes of use per day. Furthermore, brain tumors among cellular phone users did not tend to occur more often than expected on the side of the head on which the person reported using the phone.

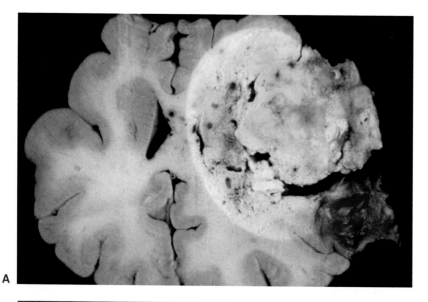

A

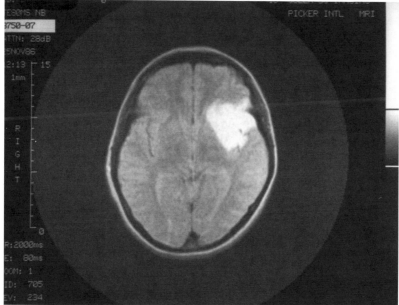

B

Figure 8.2 **(A)** A cross-section of the brain showing a tumor (lighter pink area). **(B)** MRI scan of a cross-section of the head of a patient with a glioma of the brain. **(C)** MRI scan of a sagittal section of the head of a child with a malignant glioma (shown in blue). This type of tumor is often deadly, destroying large areas of the brain.

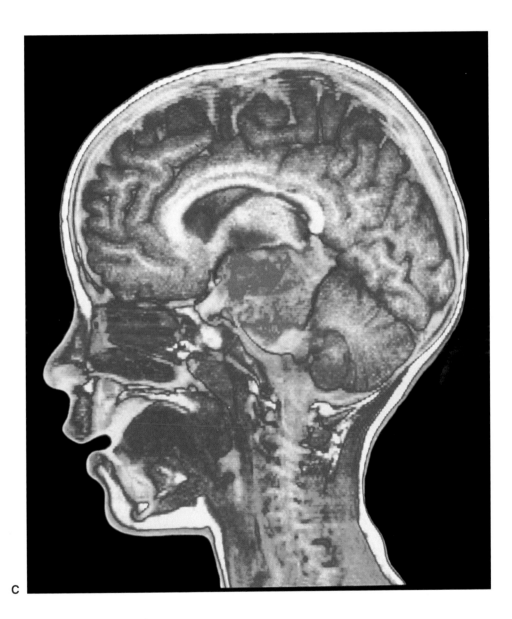

c

Gamma Knife

An advanced radiation technique known as gamma knife radio-therapy has revolutionized the nonsurgical treatment of certain brain tumors with extreme precision. Based on neurological examination and imaging studies, such as CT and MRI, this technique provides for highly accurate irradiation of deeply positioned tumors. The "blade" of a gamma knife is actually a convergence point of a large number of low-power beams of ionizing gamma radiation that destroy the tumor at the place where they intersect. Beams are aimed from different points outside the skull at a single intersection point where the beams become one.

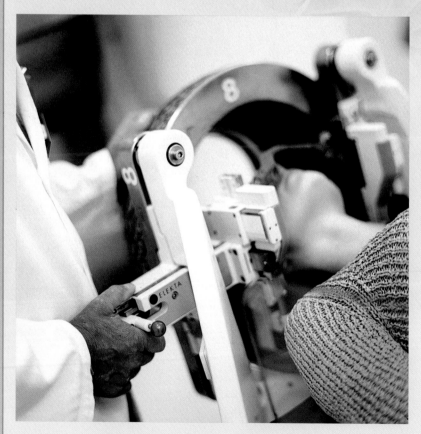

A patient undergoing a procedure with a gamma knife

(*continued from page 75*)

and destroy the tumor. Surgery aims to physically remove as much of the tumor's mass as possible without removing healthy brain tissue. Unfortunately, some remaining tumor cells can be left behind.

Targeted **radiation therapy** can be used alone or following surgery. Radiation selectively destroys remaining tumor cells, and can prevent recurrence. Radiation therapy is commonly used in cases of malignant tumors. Stereotaxic techniques use several different beams of radiation that target the tumor from different angles, all overlapping at the center of the mass. The advantage of this approach is that healthy surrounding areas of brain are left intact and undamaged by radiation (see "Gamma Knife" box).

Chemotherapy works best for benign tumors, and works by limiting cell division through a process called **mitosis**, whereby cells split into two new cells, a process that repeats indefinitely as the tumor grows.

■ **Learn more about types of brain tumors** Search the Internet for *acromeglia and tumor*, *gigantism and tumor*, or *dwarfism and tumor.*

9 | Multiple Sclerosis

M**ultiple sclerosis** (MS) is a chronic neurological disease characterized by multiple areas of damage and scarring (sclerosis) to nerve fibers of the central nervous system. MS causes a number of problems, including impaired sensation, inability to control or properly move the arms or legs, and changes in vision. As the disease progresses, people with MS may need a cane to walk or may be confined to a wheelchair, unable to perform even the simplest daily tasks such as dressing themselves, getting in and out of bed, eating on their own, or driving a car. Personal accounts of people suffering from MS describe the disease as trapping them within their bodies, or robbing them of their freedom. They describe their mental and emotional state as full of dread because they are frustrated with not knowing what the next day will bring in terms of disability.

SIGNS AND SYMPTOMS

MS affects approximately 60 people per 100,000 in the caucasion population and 31 people per 100,000 in the non-caucasion population, contributing to a total of around 300,000 MS patients in North America. MS rarely affects people of Asian descent. For unknown reasons, women are twice as likely as men to have MS. The age at which people begin to experience symptoms is usually between 20 and 30 years.

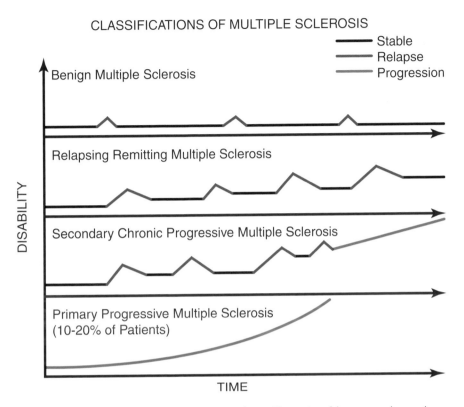

Figure 9.1 Symptoms of MS increase over time. The rate of increase depends upon the type of MS experienced by the patient.

Several typical symptoms present themselves in the early stages of MS. People often report blurry or double vision, numbness and/or weakness in one or more extremities, instability in walking, and problems controlling bowel and bladder function. Typically, numbness starts in the feet or hands. Interestingly, hypersensitivity to changes in temperature, particularly to heat, with as little as one or two degrees, is sometimes noted. Increases in temperature, such as when a person takes a bath, can sometimes aggravate symptoms.

As MS progresses (Figure 9.1), the initial symptoms generally get worse, and new symptoms appear. Blurred vision becomes more noticeable and spots may appear in the visual field. Sensory disturbances become obvious and can involve whole arms or legs, chronic pain, and severe loss of senses of vibration or body location. Motor disturbances such as weakness turn into paralysis, muscle spasms during walking become more frequent, and sometimes the individual can no longer speak properly. Balance and walking may be impaired so that the person becomes uncoordinated and normally rapid movements are slowed.

Although the disease results in progressive neurological damage to the brain and spinal cord, the outward signs of MS may come and go. The period of these attacks is unpredictable, and this **relapsing-remitting** pattern is the most common type of MS. Approximately 70% of patients with MS have this form of the disease, which is characterized by acute exacerbations with full or partial remissions. These episodes of on-and-off symptoms of neurological disruption are followed by periods of stability and partial to complete remission of symptoms. After a time of weeks to years, the original symptoms return as a relapse, or become more severe, and the cycle continues.

Another form, called **progressive** MS, is characterized by a lack of distinct episodes of symptoms, but has a slow onset and steadily worsening symptoms. With a progressive course, there is a gradual accumulation of deficits and disability that may become stable at some point or continue over months and years. In some cases, people who initially show signs of relapsing-remitting MS can later show signs of progressive MS.

INHERITANCE AND CAUSES

Studies related to the frequency of MS suggest a relationship between genetic susceptibility and environmental factors. Among first-degree relatives, the incidence of MS is as high as 20%, pointing to some genetic influence. Families that have one affected individual are more likely to have another family member who will also develop MS. The risk of people in the general population developing MS is less than 1%, while the risk to members of families who have a father, mother, sister, or brother with MS is between 1 and 4%. Twin studies show that almost 30% of monozygotic twins (identical twins who share the same egg) will both develop MS, and dizygotic twins (fraternal twins who develop from two separate eggs) have a shared rate of MS of less than 5%.

The exact cause of MS is **idiopathic** (meaning "unknown"), but based on studies, the probable cause is thought to be a combination of hereditary factors, an environmental trigger such as a virus, and a defect in the immune system. The primary mechanism underlying MS appears to involve a disturbance with the immune system (see "Prevalence of Multiple Sclerosis by Geographic Region" box).

PATHOLOGICAL CHANGES

MS is considered an **autoimmune demyelinating** disease. This means that there is a problem with the body's immune system that causes it to attack its own normal myelin sheaths that surround axons.

The body's immune system, when functioning normally, helps protect against potentially harmful bacteria and viruses. It is made up of two parts—the first of which involves the production of **antibody** proteins that attack "foreign" agents and cause them to be removed from the body. The second part is made up of specialized white blood cells that target foreign agents directly. These components work together to prevent the body from becoming sick or damaged by unknown organisms. Because the immune system can recognize the cells and tissues of the body as "self," it does not attack them. This is why, for example, the body rejects transplanted organs unless the transplant comes from a twin or the recipient is treated with immune-suppressing drugs.

Prevalence of Multiple Sclerosis by Geographic Region

For unknown reasons, the prevalence of MS is higher in areas of developed countries with a geographic position above 40° latitude, as shown in red on the map. In the United States, this corresponds to states located north of Colorado, where the incidence of MS is two times higher than in Florida, for example. Several theories exist to explain this observation, including exposure to different bacteria and viruses that live in either warmer tropical climates or cooler ones, seasonal fluctuations in sunlight that can influence the body's chemistry, and/or diet, in that some populations may eat more fish, dairy products, or other foods. Research is under way to try to understand what might contribute to the presence of MS in these parts of the world.

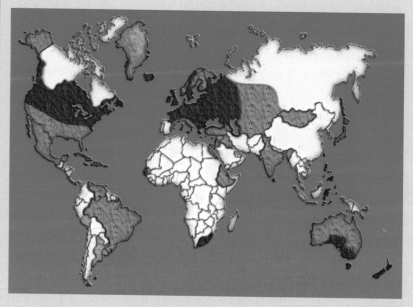

This map shows the geographic distribution of MS.

Autoimmune disorders are a class of diseases in which the immune system of an otherwise healthy individual produces an immune response that attacks its own body as well as foreign substances. These disorders are common, and other examples include rheumatoid arthritis, lupus, and type-1 diabetes. Auto-immune diseases are sometimes triggered by a bacterium or virus that causes the immune system to develop antibodies to a part of the structure of the bacterium or virus that also resembles a part of normal self cells, which are then attacked.

The part of the nervous system that is targeted in MS is the myelin sheath that wraps axons. Myelin, a material that is composed primarily of fats, is produced in the central nervous system by special cells called oligodendrocytes. These cells wrap tightly around the communicating part of a neuron called the axon. In the same way that electrical wires are wrapped in plastic sheaths, myelin serves as a biological insulator that prevents impulses propagated down the length of the axon from short-circuiting or diminishing. MS is a **demyelinating disease** in that it results in the destruction of myelin around axons. The result of demyelination is that electrical signals between neurons are reduced or completely blocked, making it impossible to relay commands from the brain to the muscles, or from the skin to the brain, for example. Normally, impulses travel approximately 225 miles an hour along some axonal pathways, but when a patch of myelin is lost, the impulses decrease to about half that velocity.

Areas of demyelination appear to the naked eye as thick hardened scars called **sclerotic plaques** (Figure 9.2). These areas further diminish axonal conduction, or, in some cases, completely block it. Breakdown products and fragments of myelin can be found in sclerotic plaques and in the cerebrospinal fluid that bathes the brain and spinal cord. Multiple sclerotic plaque formations are found randomly distributed in the nervous system, and can occur anywhere within the white matter of the

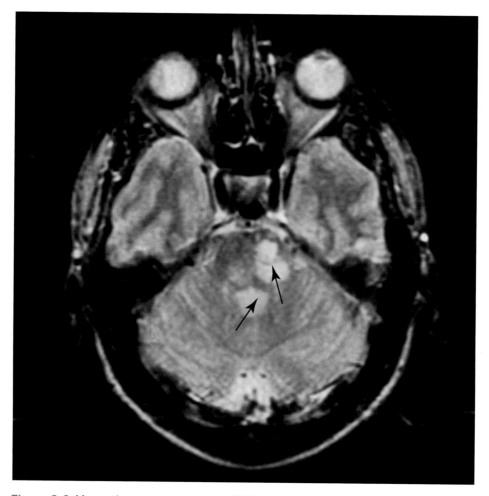

Figure 9.2 Magnetic resonance image (MRI) scan of an axial section through the brain of a patient with multiple sclerosis. The eyeballs are seen at top; regions of the cerebrum of the brain are at left, right, and lower frame within the cranium. Inside the brain (center) are a number of lesions caused by MS. Sclerotic lesions are seen as white spots in the center of the brain (*arrows*).

nervous system where myelin is present. Because MS randomly targets myelin sheaths, longer axons have a higher chance of being affected—for this reason, symptoms first appear in feet and hands, which have longer axons because they are farther from the spinal cord and brain.

TREATMENT AND OUTLOOK

MS treatments focus mainly on decreasing the frequency and severity of relapse, on reducing the number of MS lesions, on delaying the progression of the disease, and on providing some relief from symptoms. Two major strategies exist. The first main approach uses a class of drugs called **corticosteroids**. These agents are prescribed to treat exacerbations of MS in relapsing-remitting cases. Corticosteroids are drugs designed to mimic natural substances in the body, such as cortisol, that are produced by the adrenal glands that sit on the top of the kidneys. These drugs are able to reduce inflammatory reactions. During an acute relapse of MS, a significant degree of inflammation takes place at areas where myelin is being destroyed. Short-term treatment with corticosteroids can be helpful during periods of relapse.

The second major therapeutic strategy targets the dysfunctional immune system. Immunomodulatory drugs modify the actions of the immune system in relapsing MS by changing the activity of **interferons**. Interferons are a group of proteins normally produced by cells in response to viral infection, particularly interferons alpha and beta produced by white blood cells, and interferon gamma produced by a class of immune cells called T cells that promote inflammation. Interferon beta works to counteract the effects of interferon gamma, which is thought to play a major role in causing MS remission.

■ **Learn more about MS** Search the Internet for *multiple sclerosis.*

10 Other Disorders and the Future

Up to now, this book has presented several distinct diseases or disorders of the brain that affect the sensory and or motor status of the body. In some cases, such as with multiple sclerosis, stroke, and epilepsy, scientists and doctors have been studying therapeutic strategies for quite some time. Other disorders have received more attention as they have become more prevalent in the population, as with Alzheimer's disease. Several neurological disorders have received quite a bit of newfound interest.

PRION DISEASES

Because of recent concerns over what has been called "mad cow disease," or bovine spongiform encephalopathy (BSE), a human disease variant called **Creutzfeldt-Jakob disease** (CJD) has become the focus of attention because of its unusual transmissible agent and extraordinary symptomatic appearance (Figure 10.1). Both BSE and CJD are classified as **transmissible spongiform encephalopathies**, and a causal relationship between BSE and a variant of CJD, termed vCJD, has emerged. The route of transmission of vCJD is not yet fully proven, but it is generally accepted that it is spread through exposure to food contaminated by BSE. In both animals and humans, the diseases are characterized by degeneration of the brain in which brain tissue takes on a sponge-like appearance when examined under a microscope. Although CJD affects only one

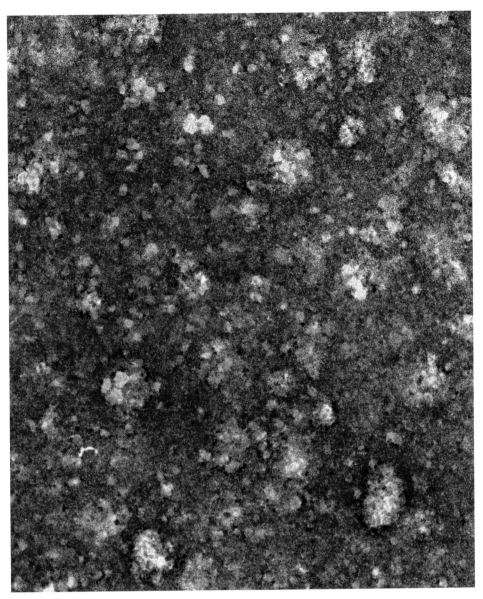

Figure 10.1 False-color electron microscopic (EM) image of brain tissue from an individual with Creutzfeldt-Jakob disease, a fatal infection of the brain. Normal brain tissue is stained red in this EM, and the infected tissue is stained green.

out of every million people, it is associated with severe, rapidly progressing neurological symptoms that lead to death within several months. People who develop this disease slowly lose their ability to think and move properly, and suffer from memory loss and progressive brain damage until they can no longer see, move to speak, or feed themselves.

CJD is caused by self-reproducing infectious protein particles called **prions**. Prions are normal components of cell structure in the brain, but for some reason they are resistant to digestion by enzymes that break down normal proteins, and they accumulate in the brain. With typical infectious diseases, DNA is required for the disease-causing agent to reproduce, and the immune system identifies and attacks the offending bacterium or virus. This is not the case, however, with prions, which have no DNA and evade detection by the immune system. For this reason, prion diseases represent an entirely new class of infectious agents.

Research has shown that the infectious prion protein undergoes a change in its three-dimensional shape, and that the distorted protein somehow induces the normal structure of other prions to become distorted. This repeating chain-reaction propagates the disease.

Another prion disease called **kuru** is present in members of the Fore tribe in Papua New Guinea who practice ritual consumption of deceased family members, including brains. Because kuru is highly infectious, the disease spread very aggressively through the Fore community during the 1960s and killed more than 1,000 people. The spread of kuru has largely been halted by governmental prohibition of cannibalism.

TOURETTE SYNDROME

Tourette syndrome (TS) is a neurological disorder characterized by uncontrollable vocal and motor **tics**—involuntary, rapid, sudden sounds or body movements. Tics vary according to how often they occur and how strongly they are expressed, but are stereotyped and occur in the same way each time. Examples of vocal tics are coughing, grunting, yelping, or suddenly using foul language. Examples of motor tics include eye blinking, sniffling, touching the ground, or tensing the abdomen. In more severe cases of TS, motor tics involve larger movements such as neck stretching or body twisting. Motor tics often manifest as obsessively repeated actions, and are sometimes self-injurious, such as lip biting. Sometimes a stressful situation or fatigue will worsen tic behavior.

Dysfunction in brain circuitry called the basal ganglia that inhibits or activates movement commands from the cerebral cortex is responsible for TS. The same region of the brain is involved in Parkinson's disease. The net result of these diseases is reduced inhibition of outflowing motor commands, which leads to uncontrollable motor outputs. In Parkinson's disease, the deficit is with dopamine-producing cells contained in the substantia nigra. In TS, recent data suggest that the **ventral striatum** and caudate nucleus are involved. The ventral striatum forms a crucial link between the movement and emotion systems of the brain, and is involved in the formation of habits and in repetitive, stereotyped movements of the face and limbs.

Drugs that act on certain neurotransmitter systems are effective in managing TS. The ventral striatum is rich in two neurotransmitters, dopamine and serotonin, that play important roles in how neurons communicate with each other. In TS patients, the ventral striatum has an abnormally high density of dopamine-containing nerve terminals. Drugs that block the actions of dopamine are able to reduce motor tics, while drugs that increase the activity of serotonin reduce obsessive thoughts and compulsive actions. A neurochemical link between TS and **obsessive-compulsive disorder** (OCD) has been proposed. OCD is

characterized by obsessive thoughts about performing a particular set of ritualistic motor tasks.

OTHER BRAIN DISORDERS

There are several additional types of problems with normal
brain functioning that are sometimes more difficult to classify
because of their perplexing nature. Many such disorders are
likely to be associated with a biochemical or anatomical abnormality, but often it is very difficult to link complex changes in
personality or behavior, for example, with a simple organic
malfunction, damage to the brain, or disease process that is
poorly understood.

Major examples of disorders with mysterious causes are
autism and psychotic disorders. A rare form of autism depicted
in the widely popular 1988 movie *Rain Man* alerted the public to
this curious and challenging disorder. Classic autism is named
after the Greek word *autos,* meaning "self," and is characterized
as a disease of social underdevelopment and withdrawal. Children with autism demonstrate extreme social anxieties such as
when separated from parents, for example, as well as hypersensitivity to loud sounds. They also exhibit stereotyped behaviors,
mental retardation, and epilepsy and/or motion disorders.
Speech abnormalities are also very common; autistic children
generally fail to fully develop language and tools of expression.
In approximately 15% of autistic individuals, extraordinary
savant abilities are present, which enable them to exhibit almost
superhuman skills, such as a great capacity for memory, skill
in mathematical analysis, and artistic and musical abilities.
There is a continuum of these abilities among autistic savants
(Figure 10.2).

The brains of people with autism reveal several abnormalities
in the arrangement of neurons in areas of the brain associated
with complex functioning, such as the frontal and temporal
lobes (involved with higher thoughts and cognitive abilities), the

Figure 10.2 The man who drew this illustration of the Sears Tower in Chicago is an autistic savant. He is able to look at anything once and immediately produce a very detailed drawing entirely from his memory.

cerebellum (involved with bodily posture and basic movements), and structures associated with learning and memory. Research has suggested that there may be an abnormality involving the neurotransmitter serotonin as well. The possible causes of autism include genetic abnormalities, complications during birth such as lack of oxygen for a brief period of time, infections during infancy, high fever, and exposure to environmental toxins.

Schizophrenia is a common psychotic disorder that likely has neurochemical underpinnings. *Schizophrenia* translated from

Greek literally means "split mind," and refers to the fragmented nature of the mental state of the sufferer. Individuals suffering from schizophrenia undergo changes in thinking, behavior, or perception, and exhibit symptoms that are characterized as positive and negative. Positive symptoms are described as being more active or expressive, and include hallucinations, jumbled and confusing speech, delusions and abnormal thoughts, and erratic behavior. Negative symptoms are more limiting, and represent a lack of or decline in normal experience or behavior, and include reduced emotion, social withdrawal, lack of motivation, and poverty of speech. General cognitive functions may also be decreased, taking the form of impaired attention, memory, problem-solving abilities, and social skills. The typical age of onset is late adolescence and early adulthood.

It is likely that schizophrenia results from a genetic predisposition accompanied by an environmental trigger. Brains of people with schizophrenia reveal several distinct anatomical changes. The brain's ventriculars, which make up a system of fluid-filled cavities that bathe the brain with a nutrient-rich solution, are enlarged. The corpus callosum, a thick bundle of nerve fibers that connects the two hemispheres, is thicker, permitting more communication between the sides of the brain. People with schizophrenia also have reduced amounts of brain activity in the frontal lobe, and excessive amounts of activity in the occipital lobe. The frontal lobe plays a key role in rational thought, decision-making, and drive, and the occipital lobe processes visual stimuli. In this scenario, the brain is perhaps receiving an overload of information that is not processed properly. Other imaging studies show a reduced volume of brain tissue within the prefrontal cortex, a region involved in memory, attention, reasoning, and organized speech. The temporal lobe also shows reduced tissue volume, which could help explain the disruptions in emotion, memory, and hallucinations. Finally, neurochemical abnormalities with the dopamine and serotonin neurotransmitter systems have been found. Drugs that block dopamine from binding to its receptor can effectively manage the psychotic symptoms of schizophrenia.

RESEARCH

It is a wonderfully exciting time for neuroscience research. Experiments aimed at understanding and correcting neurological and brain disorders are progressing at an unprecedented pace. Every day, around the world, discoveries about normal and abnormal brain functioning are being made. These studies aid in the daunting task of understanding the most complex piece of computing machinery in the universe.

Neuroscientists are studying the brain at the levels of consciousness and the mind by examining molecules and compounds and thinking about the intricacies of how neurons communicate, how the brain is organized, and how the brain acts like a computer. Questions are being asked about the brain's self-assembly, about why it does not repair itself, and why some parts but not others become damaged or dysfunctional. Brain research is expanding our body of knowledge, and aims to translate these findings into real life prevention, diagnosis, treatment, and cures for disorders of the brain.

■ **Learn more about other brain disorders** Search the Internet for *mad cow disease* or *Tourette's tics and brain surgeons.*

Glossary

Absence seizures Seizures that cause the individual to become detached from reality for a short amount of time, sometimes with muscular contractions.

Acetylcholine A neurotransmitter involved in movement commands, among other functions.

Agonists Drugs that activate the same receptor sites as certain neurotransmitters.

Akinesia Difficulty in initiating new movements and a reduced output of voluntary movements.

Alzheimer's disease An irreversible, progressive neurodegenerative disease that affects memory and thinking abilities.

Amyloid plaques Deposits of amyloid protein fragments found in the brains of individuals with Alzheimer's disease.

Amyloid protein Small proteins formed in excess in the brains of Alzheimer's patients.

Amyotrophic lateral sclerosis Degenerative disease of motor neurons within the brain and spinal cord resulting in paralysis.

Antibody Molecules generated by the immune system to fight germs.

Apolipoprotein E Brain protein found in high amounts in the brains of individuals with Alzheimer's disease.

Arteriosclerotic clots Formations of fatty deposits around the inner walls of blood vessels that break off.

Astrocytomas Tumors that form from astrocytes.

Atonic seizures Seizures that involve the sudden and temporary loss of voluntary muscle tone.

Atrophy Wasting away.

Aura Visual abnormalities that precede a migraine headache.

Autism Disorder with uncertain causes, resulting in mental retardation and occasionally peculiar abilities.

Autoimmune Class of disorders where the immune system of an otherwise healthy individual produces an immune response and begins to attack its own body.

Axon The long process that emerges from the cell body of the neuron that communicates messages.

Basal ganglia Brain areas involved in processing movement commands. The basal ganglia are damaged in Parkinson's disease.

Bases Pairs of molecules making up DNA strands.

Basilar artery Major supply artery of the brain, found at the base of the skull.

Benign childhood epilepsy Form of epilepsy found in children that is usually outgrown.

Benign tumors Noncancerous growths that do not spread to other parts of the brain.

Bradykinesia Slowing of the speed of initiation and execution of both purposeful and automatic movements.

Carotid artery One of two main supply arteries of the brain found on either side of the neck.

Cerebral cortex The outer "bark" of the brain where complex thought processes occur.

Chemotherapy Tumor therapy that uses chemicals to limit cell division.

Chromosome Coiled structure of DNA.

Clonic seizures Seizures that cause rapid, jerking muscle contractions.

Cluster headache Headaches occurring seasonally, caused by histamine release.

Complex partial seizures Seizures resulting in a change in or loss of consciousness, or entering into a trance, associated with smaller repetitive movements.

Computerized tomography An imaging technique using X-ray irradiation to look inside the brain.

Corpus callosum Thick bundle of fibers that connect the two hemispheres of the brain.

Corticospinal tract A nerve pathway that carries motor commands from the brain to the spinal cord.

Corticosteroids Drugs that reduce inflammatory reactions.

Creutzfeldt-Jakob disease Brain disease caused by an infectious protein called a prion.

Deep brain stimulation Surgical placement of an electrical stimulator in certain parts of the brain.

Dementia The loss of the normal ability to form new short-term memories, loss of long-term memories, and impairments relating to abstract thinking and judgment.

Dendrite A region of a neuron that receives signals.

Depolarized More active state of a neuron.

DNA Long strands of primary genetic material found in all cells.

Dominant allele Gene product that forces inheritance of a genetic trait or disease.

Dopamine Neurotransmitter of the brain involved in movement commands.

Embolus A blood clot that forms outside the brain in a part of the body such as the neck, lungs, or lining of the heart, and travels into the brain.

Ependymomas Tumors of cells that line the inner surfaces of fluid-filled compartments of the brain.

Epileptogenic Tending to induce epilepsy.

Excitotoxicity Process by which neurons fire at high rates, causing neuronal death.

Free radicals Atoms with an odd number of electrons that are formed when oxygen reacts with certain molecules.

GABA An inhibitory neurotransmitter that decreases communication between neurons.

Generalized seizures Seizures defined by their ability to cause loss of consciousness and rapid contraction of large numbers of muscles of the body.

Genes Fundamental instruction codes of the cell.

Gigantism Disorder that causes parts of the body to develop to abnormally large size.

Glia Supportive cells of the nervous system.

Glioblastoma multiforme Aggressive type of glial cell tumor.

Gliomas Glial cell tumors.

Globus pallidus Component of the basal ganglia, involved in movement initiation.

Glutamate Excitatory neurotransmitter in the brain and spinal cord.

Headache Irritation of the nerves around the face, head, neck, or inside of the skull or brain.

Hemiparesis One-sided weakness.

Hemiplegia Paralysis of the arm, leg, and trunk on the same side of the body.

Hemorraghic stroke Sudden rupture of a weakened brain blood vessel.

Hippocampus Brain structure involved in the formation of new memories.

Hormone headache Headaches linked to sex hormones, pregnancy, menopause, or hormone replacement.

Huntingtin Gene associated with Huntington's disease.

Huntington's disease Hereditary nervous system disorder characterized by abnormal body movements.

Hyperexcitability Increased frequency of neuronal discharges to be higher and more repetitive than normal.

Hyperpolarized State of a neuron in which the neuronal membrane is more charged than resting potential, making it more difficult for the neuron to fire.

Hypothalamus Structure deep in the brain that controls basic physiological processes such as body rhythms and temperature.

Idiopathic Unknown origins.

Immune system System of the body that protects against foreign bacteria, viruses, or other disease-causing organisms.

Inactivation Firing state of a neuron when it is being recharged.

Interferons Proteins that are normally produced by cells in response to viral infection.

Ischemic core Central area of brain damage caused by stroke.

Ischemic penumbra Brain areas damaged by stroke, adjacent to ischemic core, that may be rescued.

Ischemic stroke A closing or decreased flow in one or more brain blood vessels.

Kuru A prion disease once prevalent in cannibalistic tribes of Papua New Guinea.

L-DOPA Precursor of dopamine used to treat Parkinson's disease.

Lower motor neurons Second-order neurons in the corticospinal pathway that send commands to muscles.

Magnetic resonance imaging Brain imaging technique that uses powerful magnets.

Malignant tumors Cancerous tumors that migrate to other parts of the brain.

Meningiomas Tumors formed in the protective tissue layers that surround the brain, called the meninges.

Metastasized Spread a tumor.

Microtubules Internal structural elements that give shape to neurons.

Migraine headaches Severely disabling headaches associated with visual disturbances, extreme pain, and nausea.

Mitosis Process of normal cell division.

Monoamine oxidase B Enzyme that breaks down dopamine after release.

Multiple sclerosis Chronic neurological disease characterized by multiple areas of damage and scarring (sclerosis) to the nerve fibers of the central nervous system.

Muscular rigidity Increased muscle tone (tension) during the application of resistance.

Myelin Fatty insulating material found wrapped around nerve axons.

Myelination Insulated with myelin. See **Myelin**.

Myoclonic seizures Seizures in which an individual experiences muscle contractions only in the upper body, arms, or legs.

Neurodegenerative Causing degeneration of nervous system cells.

Neurofibrillary tangles Clusters of insoluble tangles within brains of individuals with Alzheimer's disease.

Neuron Specialized cell of the brain and spinal cord that communicates via electrical signaling.

Neurotransmitter A molecule that functions to relay messages between neurons.

Nigrostriatal pathway Connection between the substantia nigra and striatum involved in movement commands.

Obsessive-compulsive disorder Repeated thoughts about performing a particular set of recurring and ritualistic motor tasks.

Oligoastrocytoma A tumor composed of a mixture of astrocytes and oligodendrocytes.

Oligodendrocytes Myelin-producing cells of the central nervous system.

Oligodendrogliomas Tumors of oligodendrocytes.

Parkinson's disease Progressive degenerative disorder of the central nervous system. Major symptoms include bradykinesia, tremor, and rigidity.

Partial seizures More subtle form of seizures that affect sensory functions.

Pituitary adenomas Tumors of the pituitary gland.

Postural reflexes Reflexes that control standing, balance, and body position.

Primary motor cortex Region of the brain region that initiates motor commands.

Primary tumors Abnormal masses of tissue composed of the same kind of cells that make up the type of tissue in which the tumor forms.

Prions Self-reproducing infectious protein particles.

Progressive Form of multiple sclerosis that has no breaks in symptoms (remissions), and gradually worsens.

Proteins Small molecules required for the structure, function, and regulation of the body's cells, tissues, and organs.

Pyramidal cells See **Upper motor neurons**.

Radiation therapy Therapeutic doses of radiation used to kill a tumor.

Receptor The site on a neuron to which neurotransmitters bind.

Relapsing-remitting Pattern of disease expression in which symptoms come and go over time.

Resting tremor Shaking that occurs in relaxed muscles, typically in outer extremities such as the hands.

Reuptake Reabsorption by a neuron of a neurotransmitter.

Savant Someone who has extraordinary artistic, mathematical, or musical abilities sometimes associated with autism.

Schizophrenia Disorder characterized by the fragmented nature of the mental state.

Sclerotic plaques Areas of demyelination that occur in multiple sclerosis.

Secondary headaches Headaches that result from another disease or disorder.

Secondary tumors Masses of cancer cells that originate in a different site in the body from where they occur.

Serotonin Neurotransmitter involved in mood, attention, and psychiatric disorders.

Simple partial seizures Seizures in just one region of the brain, where the individual remains conscious, but experiences strange sensations, including twitching, numbness, and hearing or visual disturbances.

Sodium channels Proteins located on the outer membrane of neurons that open and close during firing, allowing sodium ions to enter the neuron and depolarize it.

Striatum Basal ganglia structures area composed of the caudate nucleus and putamen; involved in planning and modulation of movement signals.

Substantia nigra Region of the brain that produces the neurotransmitter dopamine, and undergoes degeneration in Parkinson's disease.

Subthalamic nucleus Neurons located underneath the thalamus as part of the basal ganglia, involved in movement control.

Superoxide dismutase Enzyme that prevents damage to cells by harmful molecules.

Synapse Region where an axon meets a dendrite and signaling between neurons occurs.

Tau Special proteins with microtubules that maintain stability and orientation of neurons.

Tension headache Nonspecific headache caused by neurochemical imbalances within the brain and/or muscle tensing at the back of the neck, face, or scalp.

Thrombolytic Drugs that break up blood clots.

Thrombus A blood clot that forms in the brain.

Tics Involuntary, rapid, and sudden sounds or body movements.

Tonic-clonic seizures Seizures that result in a combination of effects including loss of consciousness, stiffening of the body, and falling, followed by jerking movements of the arms and legs.

Tonic seizures Seizures that cause large muscle groups, such as those in the arms, legs, and back, to become rigid.

Tourette syndrome Disorder associated with uncontrollable vocal and motor tics.

Transient ischemic attack Brief interruption of blood flow to a region of the brain.

Transmissible spongiform encephalopathies A class of brain diseases that are passed by prions, and result in brain tissue taking on a sponge-like appearance.

Trigeminal nerve Major cranial nerve that innervates the mouth, face, and jaw.

Tumor An abnormal collection of cells that grows spontaneously and multiplies in an uncontrollable fashion.

Upper motor neurons Neurons of the primary motor cortex.

Ventral striatum Network relay center that links movement and emotional systems of the brain.

Ventricles Hollow channels within the brain that bathe the brain in nutrient-rich cerebrospinal fluid.

Bibliography

Aiken, S. P., and W. M. Brown. "Treatment of Epilepsy: Existing Therapies and Future Developments." *Frontiers in Bioscience: A Journal and Virtual Library* 5 (2000): E124–152.

Andermann, F., and E. Lugaresi, eds. *Migraine and Epilepsy.* Boston, MA: Butterworth Publishers, 1987.

Barnett, H., J. P. Mohr, B. M. Stein, and F. M. Yatsu, eds. *Stroke: Pathophysiology, Diagnosis, and Management.* 3rd ed. New York: Churchill Livingstone, 1998.

Bastian, F. O., ed. *Creutzfeldt-Jakob Disease and Other Transmissible Spongiform Encephalopathies.* St. Louis, MO: Mosby Year Book, 1991.

Bates, G., P. Harper, and L. Jones, eds. *Huntington's Disease.* 3rd ed. Oxford, UK: Oxford University Press, 2002.

Binder, L. I., A. L. Guillozet-Bongaarts, F. Garcia-Sierra, and R. W. Berry. "Tau, Tangles, and Alzheimer's Disease." *Biochimica et Biophysica Acta* 1739 (2–3) (2005): 216–223.

Brown, R. H., Jr., V. Meininger and M. Swash, eds. *Amyotrophic Lateral Sclerosis.* London: Martin Dunitz, 1999.

Camicioli, R., and N. Fisher. "Progress in Clinical Neurosciences: Parkinson's Disease with Dementia and Dementia with Lewy Bodies." *The Canadian Journal of Neurological Sciences. Le journal canadien des sciences neurologiques* 31 (1) (2004): 7–21.

Cohen, D. J., J. Jankovic, and C. G. Goetz, eds. *Tourette Syndrome.* Philadelphia: Lippincott, Williams & Wilkins, 2000.

DeFelipe, J. "Cortical Microanatomy and Human Brain Disorders: Epilepsy." *Cortex; A Journal Devoted to the Study of the Nervous System and Behavior* 40 (1) (2004): 232–233.

Doolittle, N. D. "State of the Science in Brain Tumor Classification." *Seminars in Oncology Nursing* 20 (4) (2004): 224–230.

Engel, J., Jr. *Seizures and Epilepsy.* Philadelphia: F. A. Davis Co., 1989.

Gaini, S. M. "Trends in Movement Disorders' Therapy." *Journal of Neurosurgical Sciences* 47 (1) (2003): 1–3.

Good, D. C. "Stroke: Promising Neurorehabilitation Interventions and Steps Toward Testing Them." *American Journal of Physical*

Medicine & Rehabilitation/Association of Academic Physiatrists 82 (Suppl. 10) (2003): S50–57.

Greenberg, H. S., W. F. Chandler, and H. M. Sandler. *Brain Tumors.* New York: Oxford University Press, 1999.

Guerrini, R., P. Bonanni, L. Parmeggiani, M. Hallett, and H. Oguni. "Pathophysiology of Myoclonic Epilepsies." *Advances in Neurology* 95 (2005): 23–46.

Happé, F. *Autism: An Introduction to Psychological Theory.* Cambridge, MA: Harvard University Press, 1995.

Haque, N. S., P. Borghesani, and O. Isacson. "Therapeutic Strategies for Huntington's Disease Based on a Molecular Understanding of the Disorder." *Molecular Medicine Today* 3 (4) (1997): 175–183.

Hirsch, S. R., and D. R. Weinberger, eds. *Schizophrenia.* Oxford, Cambridge, MA: Blackwell Science, 1995.

Hock, N. "Neuroprotective and Thrombolytic Agents: Advances in Stroke Treatment." *The Journal of Neuroscience Nursing: Journal of the American Association of Neuroscience Nurses* 30 (3) (1998): 175–184.

Khalid I., S. S. Sisodia, and B. Winblad, eds. *Alzheimer's Disease: Advances in Etiology, Pathogenesis and Therapeutics.* Chichester, NY: Wiley, 2001.

Kieburtz, K. "Designing Neuroprotection Trials in Parkinson's Disease." *Annals of Neurology* 53 (Suppl. 3) (2003): S100–107; S107–109.

Lallana, E. C., and L. E. Abrey. "Update on the Therapeutic Approaches to Brain Tumors." *Expert Review of Anticancer Therapy* 3 (5) (2003): 655–670.

Leckman, J. F. "Phenomenology of Tics and Natural History of Tic Disorders." *Brain & Development* 25 (Suppl. 1) (2003): S24–28.

Maier-Lorentz, M. M. "Neurobiological Bases for Alzheimer's Disease." *The Journal of Neuroscience Nursing: Journal of the American Association of Neuroscience Nurses* 32 (2) (2000): 117–125.

Mallucci, G., and J. Collinge. "Update on Creutzfeldt-Jakob Disease." *Current Opinion in Neurology* 17 (6) (2004): 641–647.

Matthews, W. B., J. D. Acheson, J. R. Bachelor, and R. O. Weller, eds. *McAlpine's Multiple Sclerosis.* New York: Churchill Livingstone, 1985.

Miller, C. M., and M. Hens. "Multiple Sclerosis: A Literature Review." *The Journal of Neuroscience Nursing: Journal of the American Association of Neuroscience Nurses* 25 (3) (1993): 174–179.

Miyamoto, S., G. E. Duncan, C. E. Marx, and J. A. Lieberman. "Treatments for Schizophrenia: A Critical Review of Pharmacology and Mechanisms of Action of Antipsychotic Drugs." *Molecular Psychiatry* 10 (1) (2005): 79–104.

Mizrahi, E. M. "Acute and Chronic Effects of Seizures in the Developing Brain: Lessons from Clinical Experience." *Epilepsia* 40 (Suppl. 1) (1999): S42–50; S64–66.

Munari C., L. Tassi, G. Lo Russo, S. Francione, R. Mai, F. Cardinale, and R. Spreafico. "Research Perspectives in Cortical Dysplasia and Associated Epilepsies." *Epileptic Disorders: International Epilepsy Journal with Videotape* 1 (4) (1999): 255–259.

Noble, M., and J. Dietrich. "The Complex Identity of Brain Tumors: Emerging Concerns Regarding Origin, Diversity and Plasticity." *Trends in Neurosciences* 27 (3) (2004): 148–154.

Ozonoff, S., S. J. Rogers, and R. L. Hendren, eds. *Autism Spectrum Disorders: A Research Review for Practitioners.* 1st ed. Washington, D.C.: American Psychiatric Association, 2003.

Robb, P. *Epilepsy: A Review of Basic and Clinical Research.* Bethesda, MD: National Institute of Neurological Diseases and Blindness, 1965.

Rogawski, M. A., and W. Loscher. "The Neurobiology of Antiepileptic Drugs." *Nature Reviews, Neuroscience* 5 (7) (2004): 553–564.

Rowland, L. P. "Ten Central Themes in a Decade of ALS Research." *Advances in Neurology* (56) (1991): 3–23.

Schiffer, D., with M. T. Giordana, A. Mauro, and R. Soffietti. *Brain Tumors: Pathology and Biological Correlates.* New York: Springer-Verlag, 1993.

Schoenen, J. "Clinical Neurophysiology of Headache." *Neurologic Clinics* 15 (1) (1997): 85–105.

Seamans, J. K., and C. R. Yang. "The Principal Features and Mechanisms of Dopamine Modulation in the Prefrontal Cortex." *Progress in Neurobiology* 74 (1) (2004): 1–58.

Segawa, M. "Neurophysiology of Tourette's Syndrome: Pathophysiological Considerations." *Brain & Development* 25 (Suppl. 1) (2003): S62–69.

Shelbourne, P. F. "Of Mice and Men: Solving the Molecular Mysteries of Huntington's Disease." *Journal of Anatomy* 196 (4) (2000): 617–628.

Singer, H. S., and K. Minzer. "Neurobiology of Tourette's Syndrome: Concepts of Neuroanatomic Localization and Neurochemical Abnormalities." *Brain & Development* 25 (Suppl. 1) (2003): S70–84.

Smith, R. R., et al., eds. *Stroke and the Extracranial Vessels.* New York: Raven Press, 1984.

Stern, G. M., ed. *Parkinson's Disease.* Baltimore: Johns Hopkins University Press, 1990.

Strong, M., and J. Rosenfeld. "Amyotrophic Lateral Sclerosis: a Review of Current Concepts." *Amyotrophic Lateral Sclerosis and Other Motor Neuron Disorders: Official Publication of the World Federation of Neurology, Research Group on Motor Neuron Diseases* 4 (3) (2003): 136–143.

Szentirmai, O., and B. S. Carter. "Genetic and Cellular Therapies for Cerebral Infarction." *Neurosurgery* 55 (2) (2004): 283–286; 296–297.

Tamminga, C. A., and H. H. Holcomb. "Phenotype of Schizophrenia: A Review and Formulation." *Molecular Psychiatry* 10 (1) (2005): 27–39.

Vinken, P. J., G. W. Bruyn, H. L. Klawans, and C. Rose, eds., *Headache.* New York: Elsevier Science Pub. Co., 1985.

Waxman, S. G. "Demyelination in Spinal Cord Injury and Multiple Sclerosis: What Can We Do to Enhance Functional Recovery?" *Journal of Neurotrauma* 9 (Suppl. 1) (1992): S105–117.

———. "Sodium Channels as Molecular Targets in Multiple Sclerosis." *Journal of Rehabilitation Research and Development* 39 (2) (2002): 233–242.

Welch, K. M. "Concepts of Migraine Headache Pathogenesis: Insights into Mechanisms of Chronicity and New Drug Targets." *Neurological Sciences: Official Journal of the Italian Neurological Society and of the Italian Society of Clinical Neurophysiology* 24 (Suppl. 2) (2003): S149–153.

Will, R. "Variant Creutzfeldt-Jakob Disease." *Folia Neuropathologica/ Association of Polish Neuropathologists and Medical Research Centre, Polish Academy of Sciences* 42 (Suppl. A) (2004): 77–83.

Williams, J. H., A. Whiten, and T. Singh. "A Systematic Review of Action Imitation in Autistic Spectrum Disorder." *Journal of Autism and Developmental Disorders* 34 (3) (2004): 285–299.

Wing, L. "The Spectrum of Autistic Disorders." *Hospital Medicine* 65 (9) (2004): 542–545.

Whitney, C. M., and R. B. Daroff. "An Approach to Migraine." *The Journal of Neuroscience Nursing: Journal of the American Association of Neuroscience Nurses* 20 (5) (1988): 284–289.

Further Reading

Cattaneo, E., D. Rigamonti, and C. Zuccato. "The Enigma of Huntington's Disease." *Scientific American* 287 (6) (2002): 92–97.

Cavenee, W. K., and R. L. White. "The Genetic Basis of Cancer." *Scientific American* 272 (3) (1995): 72–79.

Cohen, D. J., J. Jankovic, and C. G. Goetz, eds. *Tourette Syndrome.* Philadelphia: Lippincott, Williams & Wilkins, 2000.

Dajer, T. "Vital Signs: Sometimes When a Seizure Hits, Even the Doctor Doesn't Know Whether It's Real." *Discover* 21 (11) (2000).

Frith, U. "Autism." *Scientific American* 268 (6) (1993): 108–14.

Gage, F. H. "Brain, Repair Yourself." *Scientific American* 289 (3) (2003): 46–53.

Greenberg, G. "The Serotonin Surprise 'I Think You Have to Accept That There's a Structural Change in Your Brain When You Take Drugs Like Prozac.'" *Discover* 22 (07) (2001).

Jain, R. K. "Barriers to Drug Delivery in Solid Tumors." *Scientific American* 271 (1) (1994): 58–65.

Javitt, D. C., and J. T. Coyle. "Decoding Schizophrenia." *Scientific American* 290 (1) (2004): 48–55.

Miller, C. M., and M. Hens. "Multiple Sclerosis: A Literature Review." *The Journal of Neuroscience Nursing: Journal of the American Association of Neuroscience Nurses* 25 (3) (1993): 174–179.

Milonas, I. "Amyotrophic Lateral Sclerosis: An Introduction." *Journal of Neurology* 245 (Suppl. 2) (1998): S1–3.

Prusiner, S. B. "Detecting Mad Cow Disease." *Scientific American* 291 (1) (2004): 86–93.

———. "The Prion Diseases." *Scientific American* 272 (1) (1995): 48–51, 54–57.

Richardson, S. "The Besieged Brain." *Discover* 17 (9) (1996).

Richards, W. "The Fortification Illusions of Migraines." *Scientific American* 224 (5) (1971): 88–96.

Ruoslahti, E. "How Cancer Spreads." *Scientific American* 275 (3) (1996): 72–77.

Steinman L. "Autoimmune Disease." *Scientific American* 269 (3) (1993): 106–114.

St. George-Hyslop, P. H. "Piecing Together Alzheimer's." *Scientific American* 283 (6) (2000): 76–83.

Treffert, D. A., and G. L. Wallace. "Islands of Genius. Artistic Brilliance and a Dazzling Memory Can Sometimes Accompany Autism and Other Developmental Disorders." *Scientific American* 286 (6) (2002): 76–85.

Youdim, M. B., and P. Riederer. "Understanding Parkinson's Disease." *Scientific American* 276 (1) (1997): 52–59.

Websites

Ariniello, Leah. "Brain Briefings: Alzheimer's Disease and Plaques." (February 2000.) *Society for Neuroscience.* Available online at *http://apu.sfn.org/content/Publications/BrainBriefings/alzheimers_disease_plaques.html.*

———. "Brain Briefings: Huntington's Disease Genetics." (February 1997.) *Society for Neuroscience.* Available online at *http://apu.sfn.org/content/Publications/BrainBriefings/huntingtons.html.*

———. "Brain Briefings: Parkinson's and Dopamine." (January 1997.) *Society for Neuroscience.* Available online at *http://apu.sfn.org/content/Publications/BrainBriefings/parkinsons.html.*

Australian Headache and Migraine Information Site. *Headache.Com.AU: Headache and Migraine Information Site.* Available online at *http://www.headache.com.au/hachehtm/headfrm.html.*

Azari, Nina P., and Rudiger J. Seitz. "Brain Plasticity and Recovery from Stroke." (September–October 2000.) *American Scientist Online: The Magazine of Sigma Xi, The Scientific Research Society* 88 (5): 426. Available online at *http://www.americanscientist.org/template/AssetDetail/assetid/14739.*

Bernstein, Lawrence. "349 Pathophysiology of Epilepsy." *Neurology, Feinberg School, Northwestern University.* Available online at *http://www.neuro.nwu.edu/meded/m2/epilepsy_phys.html.*

Biological Sciences, University of Lethbridge. "Prions: Lecture 11." Biology 4110. *University of Lethbridge, Canada.* Available online at *http://www.uleth.ca/bio/bio4110/11.pdf.*

Blanda, Michelle. "Headache, Migraine." (November 16, 2004.) *EMedicine: Instant Access to the Minds of Medicine.* Available online at *http://www.emedicine.com/EMERG/topic230.htm.*

Centers for Disease Control and Protection. "Questions and Answers Regarding Bovine Spongiform Encephalopathy (BSE) and Creutzfeldt-Jakob Disease (CJD)." (December 29, 2003.) *Centers for Disease Control* Available online at *http://www.cdc.gov/ncidod/diseases/cjd/bse_cjd_qa.htm.*

Chamberlain, Neil. "Prions and Viroids." *Kirksville College of Osteopathic Medicine.* Available online at *http://www.kcom.edu/faculty/chamberlain/Website/Lects/PRIONS.HTM.*

Chudler, Eric. "Neuroscience for Kids." (January 25, 2005.) *University of Washington.* Available online at *http://faculty.washington.edu/chudler/neurok.html.*

The Cleveland Clinic. "Stroke." *The Cleveland Clinic Health Information Center.* (September 6, 2001.) Available online at *http://www.clevelandclinic.org/health/health-info/docs/2100/2179.asp?index=9074.*

Davis, Bowman O., Jr. "Lecture 5: Immunity." *Kennesaw State University.* Available online at *http://science.kennesaw.edu/~bodavis/LECT5.HTM.*

———. "Lecture 17: Neuropathophysiology." *Kennesaw State University.* Available online at *http://science.kennesaw.edu/~bodavis/LECT17Neuro.HTM.*

Digre, Kathleen B., and Susan Baggaley. "Headache Lecture." *University of Utah Medical Student Website.* Available online at *http://www-medlib.med.utah.edu/neuronet/headache/digre3.html.*

Fung, Dion, et. al., eds. "Gait Disorders: Hemiplegia/Hemiparesis." (May 15, 1999.) *Molson Medical Informatics, McGill University, Canada.* Available online *http://sprojects.mmi.mcgill.ca/gait/hemiplegic/intro.asp.*

Graham, Robert B. "Lecture 4.1: The Brain's Electrical Activity, Normal and Abnormal." *Psychology 3311: Neuropsychology, East Carolina University.* Available online at *http://core.ecu.edu/psyc/grahamr/DW_3311Site/LectureF/Lecture4.1/Lect4.1.html.*

Hain, Timothy C. "Alzheimer's Disease." (February 13, 2003.) *Neurology. Northwestern University Medical School.* Available online at *http://www.neuro.nwu.edu/meded/behavioral/alzheimers.html.*

Hansell, James. "Lecture 11: Schizophrenia." *Psychology 370 (Psychopathology), University of Michigan.* Available online at *http://www.umich.edu/~psycours/370-010/notes/11schizophrenia .html.*

Healthcommunities.com, Inc.: Physician developed and monitored. "Epilepsy and Seizures." (March 9, 2004.) *Neurology Channel: Your Neurology Community.* Available online at *http://www.neurology channel.com/seizures/.*

Johnson, Elizabeth. "Lecture 21: Autism" (December 1, 1997.) *Sarah Lawrence College*. Available online at *http://pages.slc.edu/~ebj/IM_97/Lecture21/L21.html*.

Lee, Steve. "Stroke: Morbidity and Mortality." (February 22, 2001.) Teaching Conference. *UCLA Department of Medicine*. Available online at *http://medres.med.ucla.edu/curriculum/lectures/Stroke.htm*.

Mayo Clinic Staff. "Brain Tumor." (July 2, 2004.) *Mayoclinic.com: Tools for Healthier Lives*. Available online at *http://www.mayoclinic.com/invoke.cfm?id=DS00281*.

Moses, Scott. "Parkinson's Disease." *Family Practice Notebook.com: A Family Medicine Resource*. Available online at *http://www.fpnotebook.com/NEU264.htm*

Multiple Sclerosis Foundation. "MS Info." *Multiple Sclerosis Foundation*. Available online at *http://www.msfacts.org/msinfo.html*.

National Cancer Institute. "Adult Brain Tumors." *National Cancer Institute's Med News*. (July 29, 2004.) Available online at *http://www.meb.uni-bonn.de/cancer.gov/CDR0000062900.html*.

The National CJD Surveillance Unit of Western General Hospital in Edinburgh, Scotland. *The National Creutzfeldt-Jakob Disease Surveillance Unit* (January 11, 2005.) Available online at *http://www.cjd.ed.ac.uk/*.

National Institute of Mental Health. "Schizophrenia—Information and Treatment." *Psychology Information Online*. Available online at *http://www.psychologyinfo.com/schizophrenia/*.

National Institute of Neurological Disorders and Stroke. "Amyotrophic Lateral Sclerosis Fact Sheet." (April 2003.) *National Institute of Neurological Disorders and Stroke*. Available online at *http://www.ninds.nih.gov/disorders/amyotrophiclateralsclerosis/detail_amyotrophiclateralsclerosis.htm*.

———. "Tourette Syndrome Information Page." *National Institute of Neurological Disorders and Stroke*. (December 3, 2004.) Available online at *http://www.ninds.nih.gov/disorders/tourette/tourette.htm*.

National Multiple Sclerosis Society. Available online at *http://www.nationalmssociety.org*.

National Tourette Syndrome Association. *Tourette Syndrome Association, Inc.* Available online at *http://tsa-usa.org/*.

Obrenovitch, Tiho. "Multiple Sclerosis (MS) & Amyotrophic Lateral Sclerosis (ALS)." *University of Bradford, UK.* Available online at *http://www.bradford.ac.uk/acad/pharmaco/MS-ALS/Oncology of BrainTumors.*

Orme, Frank. "Lecture Notes 11: The Action Potential & Nerves." (May 2, 2002.) Available online at *http://members.aol.com/Bio50/ LecNotes/lecnot11.html.*

Quinn, Bruce. "342 Central Nervous System Tumors." *Neurology, Feinberg School, Northwestern University.* Available online at *http://www.neuro.nwu.edu/meded/m2/tumor_path.html.*

Reiness, Gary. "Lecture #27: Neurological Diseases: Muscular Dystrophy, Huntington's Disease, and Amyotrophic Lateral Sclerosis". (December 5, 1999.). *Neurobiology, Lewis & Clark University.* Available online at *http://www.lclark.edu/~reiness/ neurobiology/Lectures/lecture27.htm.*

Shaw, Duncan. "Repeated DNA Sequences 1." *Molecular and Cell Biology, University of Aberdeen.* Available online at *http://mcb1 .ims.abdn.ac.uk/djs/web/lectures/repeats1.doc.*

Tourette Syndrome Chapter Webring. "The Facts About Tourette Syndrome: The Original, Although Not Official, Tourette Syndrome Web Site." Available online at *http://members.tripod .com/~tourette13/.*

Index

About the Author

Bryan C. Hains began his academic training at Stetson University (B.S., Biology), and then studied at Boston University (M.A., Neurobiology), the University of Texas Medical Branch (Ph.D.), and Yale University (post-doctoral training). Still in New Haven, he holds a faculty position in the Department of Neurology at Yale, where his time is devoted exclusively to research to understand spinal cord injury and pain-processing mechanisms of the spinal cord and brain. He has published more than 25 peer-reviewed articles in the primary scientific literature, and has lectured internationally. He has taught General, Organic and Biological Chemistry, Research Techniques, Neuroscience and Human Behavior, Pharmacology, Physiology, Ecology, Evolution and Behavior, and Physiology, Endocrinology and Neurobiology at several universities. He currently holds an appointment at Quinnipiac University, where he teaches chemistry. Hains has won numerous awards, including Young Investigator Award of the Central Nervous System Section, American Physiological Society; Caroline tum Suden/Francis Hellebrandt Professional Opportunity Award, American Physiological Society, Bohdan R. Nechay Dissertation Award, University of Texas Medical Branch; Dr. Michael Goldberger Memorial Prize, National Neurotrauma Society, George Sealy Research Award in Neurology, University of Texas Medical Branch; 42nd Annual National Student Research Forum, Anatomy and Neuroscience Award, 42nd Annual National Student Research Forum; Sigma Xi Award for Overall Excellence in Research Award; Arthur V. Simmang Academic Scholarship, University of Texas Medical Branch; Bromberg Scholarship, University of Texas Medical Branch; George Sealy Research Award in Neurology, University of Texas Medical Branch; and the Dean's Award Scholarship, Boston University. He is a member of several scientific and professional organizations, including the Society for Neuroscience, National Neurotrauma Society, and International Association for the Study of Pain.

Picture Credits